YAMORIA

THE LAWMAKER

▶▶···▶▶ Stories of the Dene ▶▶···▶▶

YAMORIA

THE LAWMAKER

▶▶꞉꞉꞉▶◀ Stories of the Dene ▶▶꞉꞉꞉▶◀

GEORGE BLONDIN

NeWest Press

Canadian Cataloguing in Publication Data
Blondin, George, 1922-
Yamoria the Lawmaker
(NorthWest passages ; 1)

ISBN/EAN 13: 978-1-896300-20-7

1. Tinne Indians–Folklore. 2. Tinne Indians–History. 3. Tinne Indians–Medicine I. Title. II. Series.
E99.T56B57 1997   398.2'09719   C97-910588-9

Editor for the Press: Rudy Wiebe
Cover and interior design: Brenda Burgess
Cover photos (from top): Bear Rock, a sentinel at the confluence of the MacKenzie and Great Bear rivers. (ComPics International Inc.) Northern lights. Dog Rib [sic] Lodges at Fort Rae, 1914. Children and drummer, Hay River, N.W.T. A peaceful evening at Bathurst Inlet. (ComPics International Inc.)

Author photo on back cover copyright Yellowknife Photo Ltd.

NeWest Press acknowledges the support of the Canada Council for the Arts, the Alberta Foundation for the Arts and the Edmonton Arts Council for our publishing program. We also acknowledge the financial support of the Government of Canada through the Book Publishing Industry Development Program (BPIDP) for our publishing activities.

NeWest Press
201–8540–109 Street
Edmonton, Alberta
T6G 1E6
(780) 432-9427
www.newestpress.com

4 5 08

PRINTED AND BOUND IN CANADA

In dedication to the Dene people of the Mackenzie Valley,
people who like myself suffered immensely through the trials
and tribulations of losses such as their land, their languages,
and most of all their way of life.

●●'·'·●●'·'·●●●'·'·●●●'·'·●●

CONTENTS

Acknowledgements/i

Introduction/v

Prologue— MY OWN MEDICINE STORY/ix

Chapter One— EVERYDAY USE OF MEDICINE/1
The Man Who Couldn't Be Locked Up.....2
Moving a Steamboat.....4
Stopping a River Accident.....5
Mind Control.....7
The Best Dog Team.....9
An Elder's Prophecy.....10
Finding Lost People.....11
Eagle Medicine Wins a Wife.....13

Chapter Two— HISTORY OF THE DENE/17
Life Before Contact.....18
The First Fur Traders.....29
The Black Robes Arrive.....35
Disease Wipes Out Hundreds.....38
Treaty Misunderstandings.....40

Chapter Three— MEDICINE POWER/43
The Beginning of Time.....44
Meeting between Humans and Animals.....48
What Is Medicine Power?.....51
How Do You Get Medicine Power?.....54
Medicine Power—A Help and a Hindrance.....57
Prayer Songs and Drum Dances.....59
Why There Is No Medicine Power Anymore.....63

Chapter Four— YAMORIA'S GREAT DENE MEDICINE LAWS/69
Dene Laws.....71

Chapter Five— GREAT MEDICINE PEOPLE/75
Mala Jeezon Meets the Creature Godene.....76
The Birth of Yamoria and His Brother Yamoga.....78
Yamoria and Yamoga Become Great Medicine People......81
Yamoria Travels amongst the Dene.....82
Yamoria and the Bad Medicine Woman.....85
Yamoria Gets Fooled by the Animals.....87
Echsone Saves His Family.....89
Medicine Power Woman.....90
Edzo Overpowers the Great Enemy.....93
Ezeetan Makes Peace.....101
Blondin Wants His Powers Removed.....104
Blondin Protects His People.....106
Blondin Travels with Medicine.....107
Ayah, the Deline Prophet.....109

Chapter Six— SURVIVAL AND MEDICINE POWER/115
Cheely Brings the Caribou to K'ahbamitue.....116
Hard Life in the Mountains.....117
Caribou Medicine.....120
Orphan Child Finds His Medicine Partner.....122
Moose Medicine Power.....125
Spirit of Fire.....126

C h a p t e r   S e v e n — MEDICINE AND TRIBAL CONFLICT/129

Yalee Makes Winter.....130

Skull Island.....132

Grizzly Bear Surprise.....134

Spirits on Goat Mountain.....135

Medicine Brothers.....138

Message from the Grave.....140

The Greedy Girl.....142

Natio, the Echo Medicine Man.....146

A Small Conflict Develops into a Long War.....149

Three Stories of Medicine Power Protection.....151

A Deadly Mistake.....152

Hiding in the River.....153

Glue Medicine.....154

C h a p t e r   E i g h t — HEALING WITH MEDICINE POWER/157

Health and Well-Being.....158

Seagull Medicine.....159

Bekah's Seagull Medicine.....161

Mucho Uses Seagull Power.....164

Unka's Curse Backfires.....165

The Swan Reveals Itself.....168

Bear Medicine Heals All.....170

C h a p t e r   N i n e — LIVING ON THE LAND WITH ANIMALS/173

Earth Elements and Animals.....174

Summer in a Bag.....175

Animals Save a Baby.....176

Bush Survival.....178

The Bear Curse.....180

The Wolf Woman.....181

Taming a Beaver.....182

Power for Dance.....184

Caribou Help.....186

Chapter Ten— HELPING EACH OTHER/189
Enemies Become Friends.....190
Sharing Ways.....192
Barren Lands Rescue.....194

Chapter Eleven— MEMORIES OF A PAST TIME/197
Caroline, a Barren Lands Woman.....198
Working to Live.....201
One Hundred Years in Denendeh.....204
A Trapper's Memories.....208
The Flu Epidemic.....211
Living the Dene Laws.....215

Chapter Twelve— INTO THE FUTURE/219
The Early 1900s.....220
Signing of Treaty 11.....224
Losing Control.....227
Claiming Our Land.....229
Making the Best of Land and Money.....231

Biographies/235

Photo Credits/239

ACKNOWLEDGEMENTS

After my father's first book, When the World Was New, *was published in 1990, many people told him how important it is to record stories of this nature. Generations of my ancestors passed these legends down orally and I recall how much I loved listening to them as a child.*

My dad's first book consisted basically of stories from the Sahtu (Great Bear Lake) area of Denendeh. He has since moved farther south to Behcho Ko (Rae), located on Tucho (Great Slave Lake), and has collected stories from many Tlicho (Dogrib) elders.

For this book, he also travelled to Hatl'o (Hay River), Tthebachaghe (Fort Smith), Deninu (Fort Resolution) region of the South Slavey, and some communities in the Deh Cho (Mackenzie River) valley area. As he travelled and talked to many elders for stories, he found it very difficult to get the number he required. This confirmed his fears that the stories are being lost. He wanted to write them down so today's youth and future generations can enjoy the stories that are so much a part of our history and our lives.

As elders pass away, so too do we lose the knowledge they have gained during their lives and the many stories told to them. Today's storytellers have a hard time passing these stories on to their children, who have so many other things on their minds. In my father's generation, storytelling was vital, but young people today are more interested in television and video games. In school they must absorb huge amounts of information, far more than my father ever had to remember. Though the time for oral tradition may not be completely gone, nevertheless these stories will have a better chance of being retained if they are written down.

Many people must be thanked for providing these stories to my father. I can only begin to name a few and I apologize if I've missed anyone. When my father travelled to Tthebachaghe he talked to Frank Laviolette, Rene Mercredi, and Father Labbat. In Deninu he talked to Alec Lafferty, Edward Lafferty, Joe Lafferty, Pete King, Gene Norn, and Angus Beaulieau. While in Hatl'o Dehe he spoke to Joanne Barnaby, Pat Buggins, and Pat Martel.

My father spent many hours talking to people in the Dogrib area. While in Tsoti (Lac La Martre) he talked to Joe Fish, Johnny Nitsiza, and Phillip Nitsiza. In Gameti (Rae Lakes) he spoke to Harry Simpson, Alphonse Quitte, and Harry Mantla. In Behcho Ko he enjoyed repeated sessions with Sammy Football, Joe MacKenzie, Pierre Wedzin, Jeremy Mantla, Phillip Huskey, Paul Rabesca, Chief Joe Rabesca, Edward Lafferty, Alphonse Lemoulle, Moise Martin, Johnny Eyakfwo, and Nick Black.

When he travelled to meetings and gatherings in the Sahtu region, he also collected as many stories as he could. Francis Tatti, Paul Baton, Alfred Tantion, Johnny Neyale, Johnny Tucho, and John Tetso sat patiently for hours telling stories. In Tulit'a (Fort Norman), my dad spoke to Paul Wright, John Blondin, and the late Fred Andrew.

Some of the artwork and archival pictures are provided by Bern Will Brown from K'ahbamitue (Colville Lake), as well as from Dennis and Joseph Kenny from Deline (Fort Franklin).

Canada Council provided funding for this project. Chiefs and Band Council members also supported my dad wherever he travelled. Individuals within the Dene Nation and the Government of the Northwest Territories assisted when they could.

The editing of this book was supported by grants from the Dogrib Divisional Board of Education and BHP Dia-Met in the Northwest Territories.

Without the support and encouragement of all these people, it would have been very difficult to complete this book. I hope the children of the future will read these stories and enjoy them as I enjoyed hearing them from my father. These stories tell how the Dene lived in earlier times; times that seem so far away from the lifestyle we live now.

Ted Blondin
March 1997
Behcho Ko, Denendeh

INTRODUCTION

Numerous books have been written about the Dene ("the people") and survival in the far North. Mostly, they focus on the first explorers and fur traders who came into Denendeh ("our land"), now known as the Northwest Territories. These books talk about how Europeans made friends with the "savages" by offering them small articles like knives, axes, and so on.

At first the exchange worked well. Dene hunted and fished for the Europeans and guided them into unexplored territory. In return they received tobacco, knives, and cloth. The newcomers wanted to push farther into the untapped North country, rich in fur animals that could make them wealthy men. They had come to make a profit, no matter what else they did.

When the first Europeans met my ancestors, they found them to be very different from themselves. Early writers have described my people as having no knowledge of land ownership and no organized government. Others said they followed game to eat and acted like animals, that they were savages. Europeans accepted this label and decided aboriginal people could not be a part of the nation they were going to build. So they cast us aside and separated us from the rest of Canadian people. We are still struggling for recognition.

Before contact, survival was a struggle because so much labour was involved in finding food and preparing clothes, shelters, and tools. Fortunately, "when the world was new," fish and game were plentiful. My people moved within the seasonal circle of life, hunting moose and caribou, tanning hides, picking berries, and gathering for ceremonies and celebrations. Storytellers say it was a time of myth and miracles, when people could communicate with animals and fly across the land in spirit form. Medicine powers governed my people's lives.

Before contact, my ancestors travelled constantly, following the caribou herds for meat or looking to find good year-round fish lakes. They were born on the land and died on the land. They roamed across Denendeh and settled nowhere. But when trading posts were built, people began to stay in one place. The traders did not feed the Dene; my people still had to hunt and fish as before, and now they had to trap fur for the trade goods that made their lives easier. Between 1750 and 1850 many Dene starved as populations of fish and game disappeared quickly around trading posts. One of the Dene laws about living off the land is to never over-harvest an area.

Traders, priests, and government men brought change to our lives too quickly. Trade whiskey drowned our confusion and muddled our thinking. Had my ancestors been given a chance to show the newcomers what they knew, life would probably be a lot different today.

Europeans judged us by their standards and that was not a fair thing to do. Even though we looked poor to their eyes, we had our own ways. We were different, but we had rules to live by. We belonged to many tribes with different languages, each one led by strong medicine people. I think I can sum up the attitude of my ancestors by using the words of a Dene elder who said, "If I can see the land, I know I'll be okay. Everything comes from the land." That's it. My people lived a nomadic hunting life and they respected the land. The newcomers said, "We see the land, now how can we get rich off it?"

This book contains stories that reflect the culture and strong values of my people that early Europeans, and non-native writers after them, missed. My ancestors lived according to strict Dene laws that are like the Ten Commandments. They were physically strong and had supernatural gifts from the Creator to help them survive. Some did not own enough of this medicine power, some had enough to get by, and some became powerful leaders because they used their great powers to help their people. Still others owned too much power for their own good and became mean and self-important. They abused their powers and caused trouble.

When the world was new, my people understood that the Creator had given them Denendeh and everything they needed to live. They did not need to travel to all parts of the world to build empires. They invented and built things to survive, and their stories told them to respect all of life. Children learned about Dene values by listening to elders tell stories about great medicine people like Yamoria and Edzo. They learned how to work for a living by watching their parents.

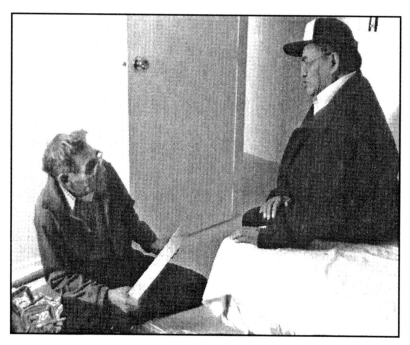

John Rebesca and George Blondin

I, too, am using storytelling to pass along information about our people that is so important to know, especially by our young Dene. They need to know the great Dene creation stories of how this world began. They can be proud of the strong values and great character of the people from which they are born. Like every other culture, we had people who were selfish, lazy, and greedy, but we also had saviours who were as spiritually advanced as Jesus and Buddha.

I hope you enjoy the stories I have gathered. Some may be more than a thousand years old; they come from another time and place so you may find them hard to understand. I have tried to tell you about medicine power as best I can, but it is hard to explain. It is a complicated subject and one that is hard to find out about; medicine people are humble and do not usually talk openly about the subject.

Finally, you may have to work out the meaning of some of these stories for yourself. Dene legends don't all have a nice beginning, middle, and end like on television. But these are the stories of my people. I am very happy to share them.

George Blondin
March 1997
Behcho Ko, Denendeh

PROLOGUE

MY OWN MEDICINE STORY

I was born near Horton Lake at the edge of the Barren Lands, east of K'ahbamitue (Colville Lake) in May 1922. When I was very small, maybe five or six years old, the spirit world reached out to me and tried to give me medicine power.

It is seventy years since it happened, but I remember the dark morning it happened as if it were yesterday. It was fall and we were living in one tent on the shore of an inland fish lake. Mom and Dad slept on one side of the tent and my grandparents slept on the other. Each day they paddled out in a small canoe to collect the fish caught in their nets.

Early in the morning, my grandfather Paul Blondin would wake me up to help him make the fire. I still recall how cold it was when we got up to dress in the darkness. He and my other grandfather, Karkeye, were teaching me traditional Dene ways and so I always had to help them do many things.

When I was a baby, I lived with each of my grandfathers for a time so they could see if I had medicine powers of my own. When they learned I wasn't born with medicine they tried to transfer some of their power to me.

My parents felt bad that I wasn't born with medicine, especially since I was their first boy, and they hoped the old ones' powers would rub off on me. In those days, if you didn't have power it was just like having no money—you were always going to be poor.

On this particular morning, everyone was up early and my mother was cooking. The woodstove was so hot that she opened the tent flap and I could just see the lake below in the darkness. Mom handed me a small lard pail and told me to go and get some water.

"Don't be scared, George; I'll watch you," she assured me. I must have looked like I didn't believe her because she added, "The lake shore is close. Look, it's just down there. Go on now." It was so dark and I was shivering, but I obeyed my mother and went to the lakeshore.

How calm everything was! The lake was mirrorlike, not a wave or ripple at all. No wind. It looked beautiful but I was so fearful I didn't want to stand and admire it. I dipped my pail in the water and turned to run back to the tent.

For some reason I stopped to look out across the lake again. I saw something! It was a giant of an old man with flowing white hair walking toward me on the water of the lake.

Now I was really terrified. I dropped the pail and ran back to the tent screaming, "Mama! Mama!" I jumped into her lap and when she asked me what had happened, I told her. She warned me not to tell anyone else what I had seen.

"You were about to receive medicine power, and you ran away! It was your grandfather trying to transfer medicine over to you. Now you have spoiled everything for yourself. You are going to need help from others all the time," she said.

We started to eat breakfast and my grandfather spoke. "He could have had medicine power but he failed. We tried to transfer medicine to him but it won't get to him. He's not fit to be a medicine man, that's why it didn't work out for him." He told my parents that he and my grandmother didn't want me to stay with them any longer.

"But anyway," my grandfather added, "I've looked into the

future and I've seen that he's going to live a long time. Raise him to be an independent man and teach him well."

It is still painful to think about how badly everyone felt for me. I felt so ashamed, as if I'd done something very wrong. I came so close to receiving my power, but I failed. I never had another chance.

Time passed, and in 1929 I turned seven and was sent off to the Roman Catholic mission school in Zhati Koe along with my brother Frank. We were forbidden to speak our own language and the priests and missionary brothers who looked after us were very strict. When I think back on those years I realize how hard life was, but I was too young to realize what was going on.

After two years, Frank and I were allowed to go home for two months in the summer, but then we had to come back and stay in school for three more years. Other students who lived close to Zhati Koe saw their families every summer. After five years at the mission school, I spoke only English and I had forgotten everything my grandfathers had taught me.

When it was time for Frank and me to return home to our own way of life, we were like aliens from outer space. We couldn't even talk to our parents because no one at home spoke more than a word or two of English. We could not understand Gokede anymore so our family had to make signs to us.

We had to learn how to make a living in the bush all over again. I'll never forget the day my parents sent Frank and me off by ourselves to visit the rabbit snares.

All of the rabbits we found were dead in the snares except for one big one caught by his hind legs. In our Dene way it is bad luck and disrespectful to club a rabbit over the head to kill it, so we tried to "pull" the rabbit's heart as we'd seen our parents do. They would grasp the rabbit's neck from behind, feel for the heartbeat with their fingers and then pull down forcefully to break the heart away from the body, thus killing it.

We tried to grab the rabbit's neck and find its heart but it was too big and strong for us and kept wriggling out of our grasp. We finally gave up the struggle and managed to stuff the live rabbit into the sack with the dead ones, then we headed for home.

When we got back, Mom hugged us with joy, proud that her sons could bring home game on their own. She started to take the rabbits out of the sack and out jumped the live one! It raced all over the tent, while Mom yelled at us. We chased the rabbit around the woodstove, spilling the water pail and breaking the dishes, until we finally caught it. My mom laughed until she cried.

So many of the things that happened to me when I was young seem funny now, but there were sad things, too. My childhood was taken away from me when I went to the mission school. Fortunately, I returned to my family and learned traditional ways from my father again. I've lived in the bush and I've worked in S'ombak'e (Yellowknife). I've got one foot in the Dene world and one in the modern world.

Through it all, my grandfather Paul's prediction rings true: I've lived a good, long, independent life, even without owning medicine power, but I've always had to work hard.

Chapter One

EVERYDAY USE

OF MEDICINE

Medicine power, you'll learn as you read this book, is complicated and hard to explain. Some medicine stories are hundreds of years old and difficult to understand, but they come from a time and place worlds apart from today's realities. To ease you into the extraordinary world of Dene medicine power, I thought it would be good to start with some quite recent stories of medicine people who used their powers for everyday, practical purposes.

THE MAN WHO COULDN'T BE LOCKED UP

Told by Gene Norn, Deninu (Fort Resolution)

A t a time when white people were first making their presence known in Denendeh, a Liidli Koe (Fort Simpson) medicine man was accused of murdering his wife. Since the Royal Canadian Mounted Police were not yet in the North, the Hudson's Bay Company manager acted as the local law enforcer. He informed the man he would have to stand trial for murder in Edmonton.

The gossip around town was that the accused medicine man had insulted another shaman in a quarrel, and not long after that the murder charge was laid on him. The offended medicine man had made his enemy kill his own wife, the people said, and now he was satisfied the "murderer" was being hauled off to court.

A few guards with the accused man in handcuffs set off down the Mackenzie River on the long winter journey to Edmonton. The HBC manager ordered that the man's legs be shackled at night and he was given no blankets, even though it was very cold.

One night the guards were awakened by the crackling of a fire. When they got up to see what was going on, they found the medicine man sitting in front of it, warming himself and free of his chains. "Why do you treat me so rough?" he asked the HBC manager. "It's so cold at night time . . . I won't even try running away." After that, the medicine man kept slipping out of his shackles.

When they finally got to Edmonton after their long journey, the guards put the man in jail and he was treated worse than ever. The cell was freezing and the man was given poor food and no blankets. One morning, they found his cell locked tight, but the man was gone. The Edmonton guards had been told the prisoner was a medicine man so they didn't bother looking too hard for him. They thought he would freeze anyway because he didn't know his way around the city and certainly couldn't find his way back home.

The snow was melting when the party finally got back to Liidli Koe. When they found out their prisoner was back already, they paid him a visit. "How did you get back?" they asked. "It took us over a month to travel here from Edmonton!" The shaman laughed and said, "Oh, I didn't have to walk like you guys. I flew with my spirit and took my body with me. In a couple of minutes I was back here."

The HBC manager shook his head in amazement, but he said, "Well, let's leave him alone. He's suffered enough. If we bother him any more he might kill someone else with his powers."

They left his home and the shaman lived the rest of his life in peace, never once breaking the law again.

MOVING A STEAMBOAT

Told by Ed Lafferty, Deninu (Fort Resolution)

Around 1915, paddlewheel boats driven by steam engines began to chug up and down Deh Cho (Mackenzie River), replacing the much slower human-powered York boats. The steamers were a boon to fur traders who could bring in more supplies and ship out more pelts in the big cargo holds, but if one of the big boats got stuck in shallow water, it sometimes stayed there.

Late one year, a man and his son rode on a steamboat making a last trip to Deninu before winter freeze-up. By this late date the water level was very low and the paddlewheeler, which draws deep water to operate, ran into a sandbar at full speed and became stuck. Crews worked until dark to free the boat but it wouldn't budge. Everyone went to sleep and early the next morning the crew was back at it, but still with no luck.

People knew the man on board had powers so the crew got together and asked if he could help.

"I will make medicine to see if I can help," the man said. When he finished singing, he asked everyone to get into the stern of the boat while he stood at the bow alone. He began to sing again and right away the boat began to move into deep water. Pretty soon it was travelling again.

The Hudson's Bay Company paid the man one small plug of chewing tobacco for getting the boat unstuck—small payment for a big favour. Still, compared to the things old-time shamans could do, this was just a little display of medicine power.

STOPPING A RIVER ACCIDENT

Told by Fred Andrew, Tulit'a (Fort Norman)

Some Dene received medicine powers so strange that they thought they would never have the opportunity to use them. Then, years later, a situation would arise in which that particular power could be used to help people. Once would be enough.

In the spring, when the Mountain Dene were travelling down swollen rivers to lower ground in their mooseskin boats, accidents often occurred in the rocky rapids, and whole families were killed. During one particular run, one of a group of boats ran on top of a big rock and swung around, stuck. The other boats rushed by, but none could stop to help because the water was too fast. The stuck boat began to fill with water and it looked as if the family inside would be swept away by the river.

An elder shouted at a medicine man who was in one of the boats to do something. "All of your relatives are going to drown! Are you just going to sit and watch?" he shouted.

The medicine man stood up and let out a loud yell. Instantly, the rock broke into pieces and the boat floated off down the river.

The people never forgot how the medicine man had stopped a bad accident from happening. They respected his powers and asked him to guide them down the river each year.

"I will guide you, yes I will," said the medicine man. "I guess that's partly why I was given these special powers," he continued. Then the medicine man explained his powers.

"I have medicine for rock. The rock that we live on, the earth, at one time was really hot. Everything on earth was hot liquid, even the rocks, and somehow I have medicine power for that.

I didn't really break that rock in the river, I just made it return to its original form.

"I also have power for water. In the beginning, when the earth was forming, there was no water at all. Then the earth fell into its route moving around the sun and it started to cool off. There were lots of clouds and steam as the earth cooled and water began to form. I have power for this water.

"But it's a problem for me," the medicine man said, "to figure out how I can use that water power to help you people now. It's possible I can use it to move big rocks in the river out of your way," the medicine man said.

The medicine man thought for a while about how he could help his people journey safely down the rushing river. Then he asked them to make him a small mooseskin boat out of three hides and to provide him with two young paddlers.

"I will sit in the back and steer the lead boat. Every other boat should then follow me. I will make a channel in the water so your heavy boats won't touch bottom," the shaman explained.

For several years he led the people down the river in this way, and during this time there were no accidents. He never had to dissolve any more rocks for the people and it was as though the Creator gave him the "hot liquid power" to use one time only, to save his people. After he died, the people missed him dearly. They were left with no one to lead them safely through the standing waves and dangerous spring rapids.

They came up with another idea to get help from one of their medicine people who could see into the future. They asked him to picture them arriving safely at their destination, when he did this they travelled safely down the river. This worked for many years until medicine powers amongst the Mountain Dene got so weak, they had to find another way.

Later on, they gathered many medicine people with lesser powers to look ten or twenty days into the future to see whether or not the group travelling down the river was still alive. When the prophets saw the people alive and well after twenty days, the people started on their river journey, knowing they would arrive safely at their destination.

MIND CONTROL

Told by Joe MacKenzie, Behcho Ko (Fort Rae)

In the early 1900s many small groups of Dene were living throughout Denendeh, making long trips from the bush to Behcho Ko to trade their furs for European goods.

One poor group of Dene had no white man's food and nothing to trade for it anyway, but as winter approached, they couldn't see getting through the season of hardship without just a few luxuries. Trade goods were like candy; people knew they could live quite well off the land by fishing or hunting moose, woodland caribou, beaver, and spruce grouse, but tea, tobacco, and sugar made life more enjoyable. So, five men decided to travel to Behcho Ko hoping the trader would give them credit.

They travelled the 240 kilometres south by birchbark canoe, portaging often. It was a rough trip and when they finally arrived, the Behcho Ko trader refused to give them credit for the things they wanted. The group began the long trip home empty-handed, meeting with another party of men who were on their way to Behcho Ko, also seeking credit for trade goods.

"You might as well turn back and go home," one of the men in the group returning from Behcho Ko told the southbound group. "The trader isn't giving anyone credit."

It was a sad-looking group that sat around the fire that night. One old man couldn't stand the thought of wintering without tobacco for his pipe so he thought hard about what could be done to change the trader's mind. Suddenly, he jumped to his feet and yelled at the medicine man in the group.

"You have said a few things about being able to control someone's mind if you have to. Why don't you help us now?" he shouted.

This medicine man didn't say anything for a while, so the old man shouted at him again. He knew medicine people sometimes had to be roused into action, and they had to have a good reason for using their powers. Stirring up emotion was important in focusing their energy so that they could activate their medicine power.

Finally, the medicine man spoke. "It's possible I could control the trader's mind in the way we want. If someone has a little bit of white man's food that I could eat, then I think I can work some medicine," he answered.

Everyone was so poor, they couldn't even scrounge a spoonful of flour between them. Then, one man remembered he had two lumps of sugar in his pack, so he gave them to the medicine man. The shaman took the sugar and went away to make medicine.

"Now, I think we should all go back to Behcho Ko," the shaman said when he returned to the group. Let's go see the trader and I will talk for you people."

Two days later, the medicine man stood with his friends in the trader's store. "We travelled very far to come here for supplies. Please give us credit, not much, just a little. We will come back at Christmas and we'll repay you with fur," he said to the trader.

The trader didn't raise any argument at all. "Yes, I will give you all an equal amount of credit," he told his customers.

The Dene returned home with what they wanted and it is said that the next day the trader didn't know what happened. He was all out of goods to trade for fur so he had to shut down for awhile.

Mind control power was valued by the Dene. It was often used to redirect the minds of children whose parents were having trouble with them. Men would pay medicine people to make women fall in love with them. Of course, mind control could be used for bad things too, like making someone want to kill someone else.

THE BEST DOG TEAM

Told by Julia Blondin, Deline (Fort Franklin)

In Tthebachaghe (Fort Smith) one winter two middle-aged shamans were arguing about who owned the better dog team. They decided to put their dogs to the test once and for all in a fifty-kilometre race to Thebatthie (Fort Fitzgerald) and back.

Abredin's three-dog team kept the lead all the way, while Rabbit Bones' four dogs followed close behind. On the way back, as Rabbit Bones tried to pass Abredin, one of his dogs crumpled in the harness like he'd been shot. Rabbit Bones unhooked his dead dog and kept on going to win the race.

The next day the Tthebachaghe people worried that contention over the race would blow up into a medicine fight. Before Rabbit Bones left for his home in Liidli Koe (Fort Simpson), the elders stopped him and told him to be careful of Abredin, who hated to be insulted.

Rabbit Bones left on the 320-kilometre journey to return to Liidli Koe with his three dogs, but toward evening a second dog died in the same mysterious way as the first. On his third day out, another dog died and his fourth dog died the next evening. Pulling his own toboggan himself, Rabbit Bones slowly travelled the rest of the way alone.

"What happened to all the good dogs you had," his people asked him when he got home.

"I had a fight with a strong medicine man in Thebachaghe and every one of my dogs died, one by one. But don't worry about me. At least I am alive and healthy," Rabbit Bones said. He could easily have started a medicine war with Abredin to avenge the deaths of his dogs, but Rabbit Bones was one of the good medicine people who didn't let things bother him. Besides, he was already thinking about how he would train a new team of dogs.

AN ELDER'S PROPHECY

In the spirit world there is no time as we know it, so medicine people can often obtain information from spirits long before an event happens. In this story, it seems supernatural beings worked through this particular elder to get his people ready for something that would have a big impact on their lives.

Around 1850, well before the arrival of the first missionaries in Denendeh, a Wekweti (Snare Lake) elder named Wheadee had a vision in which people in white clothes came and talked to him. In time, he started to pass along the advice the beings gave him. "Love each other, share your belongings and food, and always pray," he told his people.

Parents appreciated what he had to say so much that they sent their children to him for his teachings. Even people from far away heard about him and travelled great distances to hear his words. This elder made a small string of prayer beads out of babiche (a rawhide strip), and he invented special prayers to go with the beads. He composed some drum prayer songs so the people could sing for themselves and others.

Wheadee lived to be very old and was buried near Snare Lake. To this day, village people still visit his grave on Sundays to pray and ask for favours.

FINDING LOST PEOPLE

Told by Joe Nadzo, Deline (Fort Franklin)

A large group of Dene trappers left the north shore of the Sahtu (Great Bear Lake) one July long ago, to travel about 400 kilometres to Tulit'a (Fort Norman) to trade their fur. Though it was July, there was still ice along the shoreline and the cool winds sometimes tossed the small Dene birchbark canoes in the waves like paper boats.

When September came and the group had not yet returned from the trading post, the wives and elders left behind began to worry that their men had drowned. They gathered four medicine people to trace their loved ones' spirits and find out what had happened.

The shamans sang and made medicine, sometimes telling onlookers what they saw as they travelled into the spirit world. Suddenly, the shamans started to complain that the trappers' spirit trails stopped somewhere about halfway down the Sahtu shoreline between their camp and Tulit'a. They could not follow them beyond that point.

The wives and elders cried and wailed when they heard this, fearing it meant their husbands and sons had indeed been killed in the lake. The camp mourned until someone thought to ask a more powerful medicine man if he could follow the trappers' spirits a little farther.

The medicine man agreed to look into the travellers' journey. He tracked them halfway down the Sahtu shoreline. "This is where the trappers somehow lost a bearhide in the lake—one of the hides they were taking to trade," he said. "The powerful bear spirit that prevails over the lake was offended when the bearhide fell into the water, so now it is blocking our efforts to track the men.

"Someone needs to communicate with the bear from this point on to see what has happened to the men's spirits," the medicine man said. "You are lucky because I just happen to have bear power and maybe the bear will tell me what happened here."

The shaman began to sing and talk again. With the bear's help he was able to trace the trappers' spirits all the way to Tulit'a and back along the return trip. Then he began to laugh.

"Can you see that point out there?" he asked the women and elders. "If you see something out on the lake, it's them."

Sure enough, in the evening the canoes returned with all of the travellers plus supplies of tea, sugar, flour, and other goods they had gotten for their furs. That night the camp was noisy with the sound of a lively celebration as the people rejoiced to have their husbands and sons back.

EAGLE MEDICINE WINS A WIFE

Told by Gene Norn, Deninu (Fort Resolution)

A mother and father tried for years to help their only son to get medicine powers, but when no spirits appeared to him they began to think he was born to be poor.

Medicine people had investigated the boy's spirit when he was born, and they told the parents the baby had no powers. After that, the family lived alone in the bush, still hoping the spirits would find their son in the quiet of the bush. The parents knew that the younger their son was when he received his medicine, the more powerful he would be, and so they grew more worried each day as nothing happened.

When the boy became a teenager, the parents took him to sleep overnight in places where great medicine people of the past had left their spiritual powers to help future generations.

"Did you see or hear anything unusual," his father would ask after the boy had slept in each power place.

"No, I slept very well, that's all," the boy would answer.

Finally, when the parents were about to give up hope that their son would ever have power, the boy had a visit from the spirit world.

"I saw a real old man with white hair," he told his parents. "He gave me an eagle that sat down in my hand. He said it had great medicine powers. 'This bird can help you obtain any kind of food you want, almost right away' the old man told me. 'Get an eagle feather and keep it in your hat at all times. When you want food, hold the eagle feather and think of the eagle. He will do the work to help you.'"

The parents were overjoyed to hear their son had finally received his medicine. They moved back with their people and made sure they lived within the medicine laws. Happy that their son was set for life, they told him to go ahead and travel away from them if he wanted.

"But please, make sure you come back to us someday," they called after their boy as he set out on his own.

Not much later, the boy came upon a large camp of people living on a fish lake. He stayed with them for awhile and often went hunting with a group of boys his own age. It wasn't long before he started to inquire about a beautiful girl who walked past his camp each day to get water.

"That is the daughter of the chief of our people," his new friends told him. "He is a great medicine man and everyone fears him. He's so strict with his girl that no one can get close to her."

"Ah, but I would like to meet her. I think I will give it a try," the boy said, walking over to the headman's tent.

All day he sat with the family and admired how graceful and quick the girl was in helping her mother cook and sew. He spoke to no one and no one said a word to him. Towards evening, the girl's father surprised him and offered him half of one of the fish his wife had cooked for supper, and he took it into the bush to eat. Then he gathered up as much fire wood as he could and brought it to the chief.

By bedtime, the boy had decided he would stay in the chief's tent until someone chased him out. Again the headman shocked him by giving him a blanket and telling him he could stay in the tent if he stayed in one place.

The next day the boy got up early and worked all day to gain the chief's approval, pulling fish from the nets and gathering more firewood. A few months later, as winter blew in, the boy was still living in the tent, but no one was very friendly to him. The headman grumbled rough orders to him, nothing more, until finally the day came when he asked the boy to accompany him on a moose hunt.

The two found moose tracks near a hill and started to follow them. The chief told the boy to keep tracking the animal and kill it. The boy took out his eagle feather and asked his medicine bird to help him get food, and in a few minutes he came upon the moose and made the kill.

The headman was pleased with how well the boy hunted and asked him next to come with him on a bear hunt. By this time it was midwinter, when bears are normally hibernating in their dens, but the leader was a strong medicine man who could make anything happen.

Not long after they set out on the hunt, the two came upon three bears chasing each other in the hills. The headman started to chase one of the bears, whispering to the boy to stay close to him. When they caught up to the biggest bear, the animal took one look at the man and stood up, huge and snarling, while the other two circled, ready to attack.

"Do something!" the chief yelled at the boy, pretending to be very afraid. The boy threw his spear with all his might and it stabbed the angry bear in the heart, killing it. Then he fearlessly approached the second bear, moved in close so it couldn't swipe at him with its deadly claws, and clubbed it over the head until it died. He grabbed the third bear by the scruff of its neck and twisted its head; the spine snapped and the bear fell limp at his feet.

The chief built a fire close to the boy, who was preparing to butcher the animals. He wanted to see how he would cut them up. The boy worked quickly and, even though the stone knives people used in those days were not razor sharp, he had the first bear cut up in a few minutes. His hands moved so quickly the headman couldn't keep track of his movements. The chief smiled to himself as he watched and realized the boy must have medicine power for knives as well as for hunting.

The boy grabbed a bear rib and handed it to the headman to cook. Before it was roasted, he had the other two bears butchered. The chief sat back in contentment and chewed the juicy meat.

That evening, back at home, the headman was absolutely joyous as he called everyone together and announced he would give his daughter to be the boy's wife. No one could remember when their chief had been so happy. His daughter and the new-comer were an attractive couple.

Several weeks later, the boy worked up the courage to ask his strict father-in-law if he could take his new wife back to live with his own parents. Again, the headman surprised him by saying, "Go ahead. You are free to go anywhere you want. I know you can take care of my daughter."

So the boy travelled back to his parents, who cried tears of joy when they saw him again, especially because he had brought them such a beautiful and skillful daughter-in-law.

Chapter Two

HISTORY OF

THE DENE

LIFE BEFORE CONTACT

My people, the Dene, believe that we have always lived in this place, in the North. We don't accept the scientific stories about aboriginal people coming across the Bering Strait land bridge from Siberia. We believe the Creator put us here when the world was new; he put us in this place that Canadians now call the Northwest Territories and the Yukon. It is our place.

I remember well the stories my grandmother, Besiswo, told me. She said the Creator first put animals on the earth and then we humans gradually evolved from them. The stories she told me are thousands of years old and I believe them. These are the stories of my people, even if science says they are legends.

Who are my Dene people? We are people of the land; we see ourselves as no different than the trees, the caribou, and the raven, except we are more complicated. The Creator gave us intelligence to live with and look after the animals and plants on this Mother Earth, and he also gave us free will to do whatever we feel like doing.

Long before Europeans arrived in our land, the Dene lived all over the 724,000 square kilometres of Denendeh. The largest group was the Chipewyan; they hunted and fished in the Lake Athabasca area, in what is now northern Saskatchewan, northeastern Alberta, and farther north into the Barren Lands. They followed the migrating caribou and were called "Caribou Eaters" by the more southerly Cree. Among the Dene, the Chipewyan were known to have the most powerful medicine powers and smaller tribes feared them.

The remains of a Chipewyan camp have been found between Sahtu (Great Bear Lake) and Aneky Conhon (Coppermine), and there are Dene stories of wars between them and the Hareskin people of K'ahbamitue (Colville Lake), in the northwestern part of Denendeh. If you look at a map, you'll see that the Chipewyans had to travel almost 1,000 kilometres from Lake Athabasca to reach K'ahbamitue.

My own people are the Dogrib, who live between Tucho (Great Slave Lake) and Sahtu. We travelled into the Barren Lands in the summer for caribou and then went back to the shelter of the tree line in the winter, usually to a good fish lake. Today, Dogrib people live mostly in and around Behcho Ko-Edzo (Rae-Edzo), Wekweti (Snare Lake) and Tsoti (Lac La Martre).

The Slavey people are found along Deh Cho (Mackenzie River) between Tucho and Tulit'a (Fort Norman), along the Naechagah

Dogrib Indians with birch bark canoes landing at Great Slave Lake.

(Liard River), through northern British Columbia and Alberta to Hatl'o Dehe (Hay River). The Hareskin people live west and north-west of Sahtu and their main community today is Radeli Ko (Fort Good Hope). The Gwich'in live even farther north, along the lower Deh Cho in the Inuvik and Aklavik delta area, in the Yukon River Valley, and along the Teetl'it Gwinjik (Peel River).

My ancestors found their own way of survival in our land. They established their own languages, culture, and laws, the same as any other people on earth. The Creator put us in a country that was hard to survive in, but he also gave us great medicine powers to make our lives easier.

Our storytellers say that long ago, when the world was new, the weather was much colder than it is today. It was so cold you could hear trees and ice crack everywhere in the bush, yet we survived comfortably without any of the manufactured things we use today. We hunted and fished and made for ourselves all the things we needed. It was only the good, hardworking hunters who lived really well. They always had food and their wives had new hides with thick, warm hair on them to make clothing and blankets. Some tribes spent their lives moving, following the migration patterns of the caribou, living in tipis made of thick hide from the moose and caribou. Other groups found a good all-season fish lake and spent most of their lives living beside it.

Before we were introduced to European technology like guns, matches, and knives, we had to work hard for everything we had, and we developed lots of weapons to help us kill animals for food. Probably the most well known is the bow and arrow. It didn't kill an animal as large as a moose right away, and a hunter had to track his prey until it got weak and slowed down so he could get close enough to make the kill with an axe, spear, or club.

A unique Dene way to hunt was to make a snare from braided strips of hide and put it along a moose trail so the animal would walk into it and entangle itself so the hunter could spear it. Hunters

Caribou migrating towards their wintering grounds.

would also wait in small canoes on the shores of shallow lakes, waiting for a moose to come and feed; then they would chase the moose into deeper waters and then spear it.

A man once asked me, since I lived close to the land and understood a lot about animals, why the Creator had made mosquitoes since all they did was bite him and make him miserable. Not only are mosquitoes food for some of the birds we enjoy watching and hearing; long ago people used to count on mosquitoes to bite the moose and drive them crazy. To get away from this torture, a moose would often run to a shallow lake and walk in until most of his body was underwater and the mosquitoes couldn't bite him anymore. Then, if a hunter was nearby, he could easily kill the moose in the way I just mentioned. Everything the Creator made has a purpose.

The Barren Lands caribou, who travel in big herds, were a major source of food for all Dene. The people found a spot that was closed in on both sides along the migration trail and made a long fence of rocks or wood that narrowed into a corral. They set snares inside the enclosure to entangle the caribou and hold them until they could spear or shoot them with a bow and arrow.

When caribou are migrating, they surge forward in the thousands, stampeding over almost anything that gets in their way. Hunters say it's easy to hunt them when they're moving like this because they are excited and in a trance, hardly looking anywhere except straight ahead toward their destination.

Sometimes hunters waited in a narrow channel on a big inland lake for the herd to swim through and then chased them in their canoes. Once they got in the middle of the herd, their boats would be swept along with the current made by the swimming animals. Pulling up right beside a caribou, a hunter would stab a ten to twelve-foot spear at an angle into the soft underbelly below the ribs and make an instant kill. A cord was slung around the floating caribou's neck and it was carried to people waiting on shore.

Hunters also set deadfall traps to kill beaver for their meat and thick fur for warm clothing; they also caught marten, fox, and other small animals in this way. They built a kind of structure with a small one-way door and placed heavy rocks or wood on top of the frame. Inside was a stick holding bait and when the animal pulled at it, the trigger would trip, the frame would collapse, and the weight would crush the animal.

Women and children helped gather food by setting snares or using bows and arrows to catch smaller animals like birds and rabbits. Fish were also a big part of the diet, and you could catch a lot of them if you strung a net in the lake.

The only problem was we had such poor materials to make nets; you had to twist willow bark into thread and weave it into a net that was ruined if you let it dry out or freeze. You had to keep it in water all the time. Only hardworking people had long fish nets and they were always busy repairing them or making new ones. Amongst tribes who fished for most of their food, you had a lot of poor people—those who couldn't look after their nets very well.

People also built fish traps in the spring and fall when the fish were swimming to and from their spawning grounds. They built a fence with small openings across a narrow part of the river where fish would funnel through and be caught more easily. In the winter, people made holes in the ice and fished with a line and bait just as we do today.

Thick hide and fur clothing kept the Dene warm in winter, and they also came up with good ways to keep a fire going all night. They would find a big, long piece of rotten wood and keep pushing it into the fire as it burned. Long ago people needed so much wood in the winter for their fires, and they had only stone axes to chop it with, that they spent half their time cutting and hauling it.

Woman tends fishing weir, Slave River, N.W.T.

Dene who lived farther north past the tree line had to use animal fat in oil lamps to keep warm in their snow houses. You'll read some stories later on in this book about people who almost froze in the winter, but in different ways they got help to survive.

In the summer, when some groups gathered socially, and in the winter inside hide tipis, my people found time for fun and recreation. The men played handgames, an ancient gambling competition in which players form two lines, facing each other, and take turns guessing in which hand their opponents have hidden a small stick or bone.

Long ago, people played handgames to bond in friendship. When different tribes gathered together, the game got exciting as teams of up to forty players started betting everything they owned.

Games start with two people playing to determine which team will go first. The players take an object small enough to hide in the hand and put both hands behind their backs. Then they put their closed hands in front again, hiding the object in one hand. Both players guess in which hand the other holds the object. The one who guesses the wrong hand loses the chance for his side to start first.

The game is played to the drum, and drummers on the team hiding the bones beat their drums faster and faster as guesses are made by the other team. Some players wave their hands wildly and dance around to tease and confuse the guessers. When a player continues to outsmart his opponents, his movements become wilder and wilder as his team racks up winning points, and onlookers laugh at his antics.

Throughout all the laughter and high energy, someone always manages to keep score with sticks. Shouts and whoops raise the roof when a team's losing streak is interrupted by an incorrect guess by the other team. When just one of their players manages to outfox his opponents, the sticks are gathered up and the losers are back in the game.

There are stories of handgames that lasted for three days, during which players stopped only long enough to eat. People

Hand game being played by Dogrib Indians, Fort Rae 1939.

would start out betting small things like arrows and slingshots, and then move up to bigger things like spears and sleds. Later, trade goods like matches and gunshells were bet, and some people lost all of their clothes, traps, and dogteams. Today, we bet small amounts of money.

Elders know lots of old stories about how the Dene used medicine power to win at handgames. My grandfather Paul Blondin and some others from Tulit'a (Fort Norman) were once challenged by a Yukon tribe that used medicine to win sled-loads of prizes from their poor opponents. They were unbeatable and intimidated other tribes to play. After losing fifteen games, my grandfather became desperate and worked his own mind control medicine so that his opponents could only put the bone in their right hands. He guessed them every time.

When the Tulit'a team's turn came to hide the bone, my grandfather's friend sat behind his son and worked another kind of medicine power so that the boy couldn't be guessed. The Tulit'a team won thirty times in a row.

Finally, the Yukon chief stood up to say his team was quitting. My grandfather got so angry he shouted and shamed the Yukon people for being such poor losers.

The leader was afraid of my grandfather and sheepishly admitted defeat. He asked the Tulit'a people to stay while his people cooked a big feast and shared everything they had. My grandfather accepted and shook the Yukon chief's hand; then he added their food to the feast as well.

We still play handgames today, but sessions seldom last for more than a few hours and no one uses medicine to win.

Drumming and dancing was, and still is, a big part of our culture, both for enjoyment and to honour the Creator and creation. There were also ball games, and bow and arrow games of hitting a tiny target. Just like today, people always had fun seeing who had the most luck and skill to win a contest.

Education was important for survival. Elders played a special role teaching children and youth about Dene laws and telling stories that held important lessons of how to live. Children watched their parents work and helped them; they learned how to make a living and then married and started their own families.

So, from my telling you a bit about my ancestors, you can imagine how difficult it was to stay alive long ago in Denendeh. Fortunately, everyone owned at least a little bit of medicine power to help them get by. The winters were the worst, of course, they were long and my people had poor tools to hunt animals and gather food. For example, their bone chisels often broke when they tried to drill holes in the ice to fish. If they were lucky, someone with medicine for fish would come along and help feed everyone.

here is a story about a medicine man who wanted to make a good fishing place for the people near Deline (Fort Franklin). At a spot at the head of Sahtu De (Bear River) where the water naturally stayed open about three miles out into Sahtu (Great Bear Lake) all winter, he made medicine. He placed permanent trout and herring bait there, so people could make a hole in the ice close to the open spot and spear as many fish as they needed. Lots of people passed by this way on their way to Tulit'a to trade their furs twice a year, and the people of Deline shared their fish with them. Even today, there are still lots of fat fish at that place in the lake.

Another man had duck medicine; storytellers say ducks passing overhead recognized him as their leader. He lived on a big fish lake where ducks and geese paid their respect to him. Little ducks landed in the water for a time and the bigger swans and geese cir-

Colville Lake Indian hunting caribou in winter.

cled overhead and honked greetings. People claimed they could hear this man mumble words in duck language and then he would laugh with joy as he communicated with them. This man became chief of his tribe because the people knew if they stayed close to him they would never starve. Before he died, this man made medicine for duck food to grow near the fish lake so that, every spring, the people would have lots of ducks to kill and eat.

My ancestors lived in a magical time, when things that are unheard of today happened all the time. They spoke to animals, they could "fold up" the land and travel great distances in seconds, or tell a person about the past lives she had already lived by reading her spirit. The people had different beliefs in what was possible, and so they took for granted the things we would consider strange or simply impossible. The expectancy and desire of the whole tribe was behind a shaman; this power of thought also helped miracles to occur.

This mystical world lasted for thousands of years until the Europeans arrived on this continent. There are many explanations for the disappearance of medicine power. I think as people relied more on European trade goods than themselves to survive, and became Christianized, the ceremonies were abandoned and old ways of power died. The Creator saw the Dene no longer needed medicine and so it was taken away.

THE FIRST FUR TRADERS

istory books tell us the first traders in northwestern Canada found their way from the shore of Hudson Bay up the Nelson River to get to Lake Winnipeg in 1670. There, they traded with the Cree and Sioux for many years. As early as 1717, a trading post was established at the mouth of the Churchill River. Hudson's Bay Company records show that between 1719 and 1735, as many as sixty-two "northern Indians" per year were visiting the fort to trade. Some Dene from the Tucho area travelled over 640 kilometres to get the wondrous metal knives, axes, and needles they'd seen or heard about.

The huge Chipewyan nation was the first to become really involved with the fur traders, and they became agents between the Company and smaller Dene tribes who brought them furs for trade. To gain this position for themselves, they first had to fight with the Cree who had travelled west with the first traders and who didn't want rivalry. After peace was finally made between the Cree and Chipewyan years later, the traders had to persuade the Chipewyan not to dominate the fur trade and to let other tribes participate. They didn't want competition from any intermediate agents at all, preferring instead to keep all the profit for themselves.

The Churchill River Post traders were kept so busy, many years passed before a few brave whites ventured up the Churchill River and across Methey Portage to reach the Athabasca River. They found the northern lands rich in fur. In 1786, Cuthbert Grant, of the

Northwest Company, and Lauren Leroux, of Gregory McLeod and Company, established a trading post on the south shore of Tucho. It attracted Dene from Behcho Ko (Fort Rae) and as far as Liidli Koe (Fort Simpson). By 1794, only the Northwest Company remained. Its central post was by this time on Moose Deer Island, now Mission Island, close to the present site of Deninu (Fort Resolution).

In 1788, Tesiatanie (Fort Chipewyan) was established at the east end of Lake Athabasca. Alexander Mackenzie used it as a base for his explorations up Deh Cho the following year. He found tribes still living in the stone age. It would be almost a century before a trading post would be built at Radeli Koe, located far up Deh Cho to the North. Because people living in isolated regions of the North had limited European contact, they remained closer to their Dene culture. To this day they have more storytellers than the southern tribes.

By the early 1800s European traders had convinced the Chipewyan to allow other tribes to trade freely at Lake Athabasca and business boomed. The Northwest Company and the Hudson's Bay Company competed fiercely for the Dene to trade with them and skirmishes and fights between the white traders resulted in many deaths.

By 1850 a Catholic Mission was serving Tesiatanie. Fort residents grew potatoes, carrots, and turnips in the sandy soil and had a good meat supply in the plentiful ducks and muskrat residing in the delta. More and more white people and Metis were drawn to Tesiatanie, many of whom went on to establish trading posts throughout the North.

In those early days, the traders used French Canadian voyageurs to transport supplies across the vast country in freighter canoes that could carry up to thirty fur bales and a crew of five to eight men. Strong backs and shoulders carried eighty-six-kilogram packs, and canoes, over long portages. It's no wonder the traders wanted about a hundred beaver pelts for a cheap muzzle-loader gun. Twelve steel needles cost one beaver pelt. My people say in the

Trading steamer bringing supplies to Fort Resolution.

beginning the traders never had enough to supply our demands and so they charged enormous amounts for the knives, axes, tea, tobacco, guns and lead balls they brought.

Storytellers say large families could only buy five bullets a year, that's how tight things were. If a hunter missed the animal he was aiming at, he had to look around in the deep snow for his lost bullet! There are many, many stories of how the traders cheated the Dene by charging them too much, but we really didn't know the value of fur back then.

As the fur trade grew, Deninu (Fort Resolution) was built to serve the Tucho Dene. The Deninu area was a big gathering place in the mid-1800s and at one time there were more than ten freetraders there, all competing for business. Some were so desperate for business they would load up a toboggan with provisions and head into the bush to trade for fur before the Dene could get to town. Many

Dene passed through Deninu and lots of stories about medicine power come from there.

With the incoming traders came the Metis, the offspring of aboriginal and European parents. Traders employed many as voyageurs, interpreters, food providers, and freight haulers, and they sometimes struck out on their own as trappers and hunters like the Dene. Their lifestyle and culture were also a mixture; they loved European fiddle music and step-dancing, along with Native drum dancing and handgames. Some Metis worked their entire lives on the Slave and upper Athabasca rivers, piloting the early York boats and then later the steam and diesel boats up and down Deh Cho. The Metis are a very important part of Denendeh history and dozens of family names like Beaulieu, Mandeville, Lafferty, and Mercredi live on.

As more and more Europeans discovered the North's riches, transportation improved. As early as 1788, the Hudson's Bay Company freighted goods in a fleet of large, flat-bottomed York boats, propelled by voyageur oarsmen. These boats carried loads from Fort Chipewyan up the Slave River to northern destinations like Tthebatthie (Fort Fitzgerald), Deninu, and up Deh Cho as far as the Arctic coast. Heading west and south, York boat brigades brought supplies down the Peace River to Dunvegan and into British Columbia. Experienced men guided boats through rapids, or organized portages if the current was too dangerous.

By 1910 steamboats were chugging up and down the Slave and Peace rivers, and later the Deh Cho. A railroad, built between 1912 and 1914, linked Edmonton to Athabasca Landing as government became interested in developing the North.

The steamboats carried cotton thread for fish nets, metal dishes, cloth, blankets, and canvas tents, to mention only a few of the things that made life easier for the Dene. No longer did the wives of successful trappers have to do the long, tedious work of tanning animal hides for clothing and shelter. They could afford to buy such luxuries as treadle sewing machines so they could make their family's clothing, and flannel to make diapers so they didn't have to use mossbags for their babies.

In 1925 the first outboard motors were shipped to Liidli Koe (Fort Simpson), Tulit'a (Fort Norman) and Radeli Ko (Fort Good Hope). Only good trappers could afford to buy them but with these motors they could travel to more fishing spots in a day than they could in a week before. The three-horsepower motors made a lot of noise; people didn't know what to think of them at first.

Saws, nails, and special tools were freighted north and trappers learned to build better houses for their families. Even though we relied on the land to supply most of our food, we soon acquired a taste for coffee, rolled oats, dried fruit, and eggs. People were wild with excitement about the first boat that came up Deh Cho every spring because it carried the oranges they enjoyed so much.

Unloading boats at Fort Resolution, Great Slave Lake.

Instead of hunting to feed ourselves, the Dene became trappers as well so we could buy all these wonderful new things that made our lives so much easier. Our direct link to the land for everything we needed was starting to become a little weaker as we bought more and more from the store and abandoned our old spiritual beliefs for Christianity.

THE BLACK ROBES ARRIVE

In 1852 French Oblate Father Faraud arrived in Deninu (Fort Resolution) and by 1856 a mission served nearby Moose Deer Island. The first priests had a hard time converting my people to Christianity. We lived in the bush and were always moving so we weren't interested in coming to church. But gradually, as more and more time was spent near the trading posts and missions, my ancestors became naturally curious about the Black Robes and their ceremonies. The silk vestments the priests wore and the gold chalices they used to serve communion captured their attention.

When the first missionaries came, talking of a powerful God and of heaven, my people respected them, thinking they must have great medicine powers because their Dene spiritual leaders had often received their powers through similar visions. We easily accepted Bible stories about miracles and saints who helped people. The priests spoke of God, a great being who helped us and wanted us to love each other, and these early teachings did not go against our own Dene laws. My people were poor and gladly accepted any help the church could offer in the way of food and blankets. They liked to hear about this God who would look after them, this God for whom the priests worked.

But the priests believed Christianity was the only religion to live by and told us our culture was evil. They preached that we would burn in hell forever if we kept singing with our drums and offering food to the fire. They told us to stay away from ceremonies and not to listen to our medicine people.

The priests worked hard to spread the Christian message and by 1890 there was both a Catholic and Anglican mission at Deninu. My people looked at Christianity as a new adventure and were excited to come to church. Gradually, they turned away from their traditional ways toward Christianity. They would travel hundreds of kilometres to have their children baptized so they could enter the Kingdom of Heaven after death. Christmas mass was the most important event of the year to many families.

When the mission schools began to educate our children, talk of Dene culture and medicine power was forbidden. The nuns and priests said it was of the devil. We spent most of our days kneeling in church. We were not allowed to speak our language and children who were taken away to mission schools became like strangers to their parents. Elders ceased teaching young people about the old ways.

By 1920 most Dene had converted to Christianity, but some kept on praying with the drum and following their culture. Most priests didn't like that, but how could they control what we did when we were out on the land? The Catholic Church has since realized its error. When the Pope came to Liidli Koe (Fort Simpson) in 1986, he asked the bishop to ask us for forgiveness for imposing Christianity on our people.

"God put you here in the first place with everything you needed and with your own spiritual way of praying to the Creator. We came and tried to break your culture. It was wrong. Please forgive us," the bishop said to us. After that, we started to bring our drums and sing prayer songs in church.

Steamboat, missionaries, and children.

DISEASE WIPES OUT HUNDREDS

ickness was also responsible for the loss of our Dene culture. In 1884 and 1920, flu epidemics brought to the North by white traders killed many people. The worst loss came in 1928, when the steam boats carried the dreadful virus all the way to the Arctic coast. The Dene say flu killed half of their population in the Deh Cho Valley.

By this time Treaty 11 was signed and the federal government was beginning to exploit the North, drilling for oil and developing mines. The government promised us compensation by looking after the health, education, and welfare of the Dene, but these promises failed us miserably. We had no doctors or nurses to treat this sickness and so death swept the North. Storytellers say Chipewyan medicine people helped some people survive the disease with medicine they made from skunk bladders, but it wasn't enough. Desperate people nailed skunk hides on their door frames, believing the disease was scared of the animals, but the flu raged on.

Elders believe the 1928 epidemic happened because we were weak from living the white man's way and the fact people were misusing what little medicine power we had left. They also say that two very strong shamans, who were at a feast in 1926 in Tulit'a (Fort Norman), quarreled over who was to blame for a murder and then threatened to kill each other. One said to the other, "If you kill me, I will take all the medicine people still living today away with me!" On the third morning after the argument, one medicine man died and the other passed away in the evening. They killed each other and then the flu epidemic came two years later to wipe out everyone, even strong medicine people.

Though Treaty 11 was signed in 1921, it took the government another twenty years to come through with some of the promises made in the agreement. By this time, tuberculosis was out of control and many died from it. The government health department tried to prevent the disease from spreading and ruled that no one who had TB could stay in the community. RCMP officers would drag mothers, fathers, or children out of their tents and send them to Edmonton sanitariums. No one understood what the government was doing. People cried as loved ones were taken away, many never to be seen again. Many died and were buried in the south. Others were separated from their families for up to six years while they were being treated.

By 1940, four of the North's larger centres had hospitals, while nursing stations were built in smaller communties. Today, many Dene act as medical assistants and health services are good, but only after we have suffered great loss.

TREATY MISUNDERSTANDINGS

reaty 11 was misrepresented and quickly passed because oil was found at Le Gohlini (Norman Wells), and later in the Sahtu area, pitchblende was discovered; it was used to make the first atomic bombs. Most of my people couldn't write or read, yet they were coerced into signing documents they knew nothing about. Federal officials knew they'd better get title to the land from us quickly so we wouldn't stand in the way of all the money to be made from natural resources.

Big promises were made to entice us to mark our "X's" on the official papers. In addition to education, health care, and social welfare, we were also promised an annual five dollar treaty payment, for these promises we gave away our birthright.

We were left to our sickness and poverty between the 1920s and 1940s. No one came around to help us. Fur prices dropped, there were no jobs, and we lived in despair. We depended on the Hudson's Bay Company and the missionaries, but they didn't help us much. Gone, too, were the medicine powers we had once relied on.

To make things worse, the government built schools to educate our children, and decreed every child had to attend. Families could no longer stay in the bush to trap furs because their children had to be in school. The government built houses so people could stop living in tents and told us we had to eat well. How were we expected to pay rent and buy food if we couldn't get out on the land to trap and make money? Even if we lived in town and tried to get work, the big mining and oil companies wouldn't hire native people; there were no equal opportunity programs back then. Even though we were swept up in modernization, our Dene lifestyle continued to clash with the new world.

We met with the government to ask for help. Officials responded by giving social assistance to families who had schoolchildren. The government meant well, but that assistance dealt us a deadly blow. Our self-dependence, self-worth, and pride evaporated as we learned to rely on the government system of payments. Our self-esteem and power were being taken away.

From the 1950s to the 1980s, alcohol numbed the pain my people felt from all that had been taken away from them. People who drank couldn't go to work or school; many ended up in jail for crimes they committed while intoxicated. It was our children, though, who suffered the most. Family closeness—the learning and

American Camp building pipeline.

sharing system that had always been such a big part of Dene culture —was broken apart. We wandered in darkness.

Today, the cloud has lifted a little, but politics and other realities continue to challenge us. Involved in land claims and a battle for our own self-determination, we are making a bid to gain back our self-esteem, cultural values, and pride.

I hope this book will help us to gain back our personal power. I want it to remind us of traditional knowledge, of the old ways, and how the Creator and the earth once helped us to live our lives well. We need to trust in those ways again.

Chapter Three

MEDICINE

POWER

THE BEGINNING OF TIME

The great Dene stories of the past, when the world was new, go back to the beginning of human existence on this earth, when the Dene were partly animal. This is why storytellers have no problem talking about humans being able to talk to animals, birds, and fish.

I'm going to use a little bit of scientific information here to talk about the creation of our planet and how these theories relate to Dene stories about medicine power. Some millions of years ago the earth was just a ball of fire. It was much like the sun, wandering around in space until it fell into travelling a route around the sun we have today. It took a long time, but the earth finally began to cool off. This cooling created a fog, like the clouds of today, which produced rain and helped water to appear on this earth.

The Dene stories we have about the beginning of time are very vague, but here is one about medicine power that relates to the earth when it was a ball of fire.

Long ago, two great enemies met in an argument about a moosehide and a knife. One of the men wanted the big knife that belonged to his opponent. In the course of the argument a fight erupted and the knife owner made a move to stab the other man with it. They moved into fighting position and were locked in battle; the knife owner had only to push the knife into his opponent's belly to kill him.

Suddenly his enemy invoked his medicine power that could melt anything. "In the beginning, when the earth was a ball of fire, all things were melted, just liquid," he said. When he got the words out, the knife immediately melted into water and dripped down the knife owner's hand. The knife owner became frightened and ran away.

The shaman who made the knife melt had medicine for heat and melting things, a natural element on this earth. Since he had medicine for this melting, he used special words to call this power to him to help him at a time when he really needed it. You'll learn more about how people could do this long ago in later stories.

Scientists say it rained on this earth for hundreds of years; rivers and lakes started to form. In that water, insects began to grow. Eventually, the rivers cut through the rock that was once on fire and

Northern lights.

soil was produced. In that soil, plants began to grow and then insects emerged from the water and began to live on the land.

Fish grew in the water and then adapted themselves to live on land, creating the earth's first land animals. From these animals, specifically the monkey, scientists say human beings evolved.

Dene stories say we came from animals, but the legends I have heard don't say which animals. I do know that our people used medicine power to find answers about our early existence, but so many of them were silent about what they knew. Their medicine power did not allow them to talk about it. Of course, a lot of people who didn't know anything about the subject made up their own stories, things not revealed to them through medicine, and so led people astray. If knowledgeable medicine persons tried to explain how the universe functioned, by relating the source of their power to the earth's beginning, to the moon, or to the other eight planets, people often didn't believe it anyway.

I once heard of a man who used his medicine, that related to a planet, to win in hand games. After he had won everything in the guessing and betting game, he tried to explain a little about his medicine and that there are nine planets circling the sun in space. He explained that the earth is round and spinning, but he didn't word his teachings very well. No one understood what he was trying to explain.

Medicine power long ago was so strong it was capable of transforming animals into human beings. There is a story you will read later about a woman who gave birth to wolf cubs, and another about a boy who didn't like being human so he went back to being a caribou. When he found he didn't like being a caribou, he became a man again.

Many old medicine stories talk about giant animals—bats, dinosaurs, beaver, monkeys—which once roamed the earth. Storytellers say we came from animals and long ago there were many half-animal/half-human life forms. It seems during this period that genetic forces as we know them today were out of control.

Two old storytellers in Tulit'a (Fort Norman) told me that a long period of time passed before human beings developed. They talked about overgrown, semihuman monsters that wandered about on the land. They had their own language and a very rugged way of life. Maybe that is what sasquatches are. The storytellers seem to be talking about the stone age, a terrible period when there were no laws, no control and people killed each other and ate each other when they were starving. There was no such thing as working together; some groups probably survived by hiding themselves and using medicine to protect themselves. It's possible this period lasted thousands of years until Yamoria, whose name means "one who travels around the earth," came along and established law and control so people could improve their lives.

MEETING BETWEEN HUMANS AND ANIMALS

A story that involves Yamoria tells of a conference that once took place between animals and humans:

W hen the world was new, animals and humans held a conference to see how they would relate to each other. Yamoria used medicine power to control everyone's mind to arrive at a fair resolution. The meeting lasted a long time and involved humans and every bird, fish, and animal that lived on the earth. All agreed that humans could use animals, birds, and fish for food, providing that humans killed only what they needed to survive and treated their prey with great respect. Humans must use every part of the animal and never waste anything.

It was also made law that humans take the bones of the prey and place them in a tree or scaffold high above the ground. And finally, humans were told to always think well of animals and thank the Creator for putting them on the earth.

When the conference was over, communication was still possible between humans and animals, especially when medicine people needed to talk to animal leaders regarding issues not resolved at the conference. Slowly, communication between the two life forms dwindled, until today it is rare to find someone who can talk to animals.

At face value these stories about powers coming from earth forces and human beings developing from animals seem impossible because we can't imagine these things having any relation to our world today. But we must consider several matters here, and I think we can understand two things from such stories.

The first consideration is that every creation in the universe is a bundle of pure energy. Long ago, the Creator gave human beings, who are also energy forms, medicine powers to call upon these forces to help us. This supports the Dene belief that everything in the universe is connected, like a string of beads. We just have to know how to tug on those beads to get an energy form to help us, like the wind, rain, or the melting force of the fire on earth when it was a burning mass.

The second matter concerns the spirit. We human beings must be pure spirit if, at one time, we were able to change from a human

(Photo: ComPics International Inc.)

Caribou migrating towards their wintering grounds.

being, to a caribou, and back again. We must be more than our bodies if, as you'll read in stories to come, we were able to travel in spirit to talk to animals to beg them to help us survive.

From our Dene ancestors, we learn we are more spirit than physical. We took on this physical body so we could learn what we need to know on this earth regarding emotions and compassion and being kind and loving people. When we die, we can graduate into the spirit world, and help other energy forms still struggling with their emotions of hatred, greed, and envy.

This has been explained many times about aboriginal people in many books but I think it's important to repeat it once more. When the Dene or other nations pray to an eagle or bear or some other animal, we are not praying to that animal. Rather, we are addressing the spirit of that animal—trusting that the energy of the special gift that animal owns (such as the bear's power to heal wounds or the eagle's keen eyesight, or foresight to see ahead and prepare accordingly) will help us.

We have come a long way in the wrong direction, I think, from what our ancestors knew about spirit and energy. We are so much more than just our physical forms. We need to remember we are all connected and everything the Creator has made will respond to us.

WHAT IS MEDICINE POWER?

When the world was new, everything was based upon medicine powers. Dene storytellers say our existence depended on it. It's the only thing that our ancestors believed could help them, so it was supremely important to them.

Today, it's difficult to try to define this subject. The best I can do is say that medicine power is a spirit, with a mind of its own, and it attaches to us or, to see it another way, we borrow it. A person can't control this spirit. It comes with its own rules or policy, so the owners have to follow those orders and live carefully by them, or they could be killed by their own medicine powers.

Medicine people are special and live differently from everyone else because they follow strict medicine power rules. One of the most common rules accompanying medicine power is that the owner does not talk about his abilities. That is why we know so little about medicine and, even today, I found it hard to talk to elders about the subject because they were instructed not to say anything about it. A lot of shamans had a great deal to teach us, but they could never tell what they knew without losing it.

Medicine power cannot be measured and you never know how much a person has. Because it is spirit, medicine power will not die and it has its own "mind," separate from its owner. When medicine people get old and are ready to die, their powers often leave them and the shaman becomes an ordinary person again. Often a person with powers will call a special loved one to their deathbed and tell them the secrets they have protected all their lives.

When they leave a dying person, those powers immediately start looking for a baby to be their new owner and to become a shaman. Medicine power moves in cycles, and can reincarnate in new bodies, just as the Dene believe our spirits can take on new bodies and return to earth after we die.

I hope the legends and stories I have gathered here will paint a picture of the wide range of medicine power, and help you to gain some understanding of it from them.

In the beginning, all humans, birds, and animals possessed medicine powers. These powers were put on the earth so that all life forms could look after themselves. Storytellers don't say where the powers came from, but it's possible the Creator made them.

Today, many of these stories are hard to believe. Strong medicine people or shamans could create storms and bad weather to hide under so they could get close to a moose or caribou and kill it with a bow and arrow. Others could produce a lot of rain to put out forest fires, or stop land slides. Some had powers from the essences of wind, cloud, air, sun, moon, and other planets in space.

The Creator gave these powers to individuals to be used only when they were absolutely needed for the survival of the Dene. A shaman who had wind power might be able to make the wind blow in any direction so he could always be downwind of a moose and so be able to make a kill successfully. Wind power might also be called upon to fill the sail on a canoe so the medicine man could travel someplace quickly.

Some medicine people could break rock, just by pronouncing the wording connected with the power. Some could make the weather milder if it was too cold for a long period of time. Some could force heat from the sun.

There are a few cases in which powerful shamans buried themselves in rocks or mountains, and these are landmarks many Dene still know about today. Possibly, some of these shamans still have

View from the rugged summit of Bear Rock.

their powers locked in these landmarks and give them out to young people who seek them, if they are the right ones.

Strong medicine people knew how the earth and the heavens operated and how to tap their forces. It seems that their powers came from energy or natural forces on the earth and in the universe, powers placed there by the Creator.

HOW DO YOU GET MEDICINE POWER?

There are three ways in which an individual can receive medicine power. In the first, you receive it before you are born. This is the best way to get it; your powers are strongest this way. If you receive medicine power this way, you were picked to be a shaman. You don't even have to work for it. The Great Spirit, or God, has looked ahead in time and decided you will be capable of owning and dealing with such supernatural abilities. Your spirit will have received the powers even before you were born.

Your life is very interesting when you learn you are the owner of these powers. You are capable of accomplishing a lot with them, but you must follow the strict laws of your power and you're not free to do anything you like. Actually, your life can be dangerous if you overdo things and come into conflict with your powers. You could die early.

Strong medicine people gave the Dene rules to follow for everyone's well-being, like "you should share what you have" and "never gossip or say bad things about anyone." The people who received powers before birth were not always good people and they didn't have to follow these good rules. They had the power to kill anyone they wanted. Sometimes, they got proud and gave weaker people a hard time. They were given powers to help the poor, but sometimes they got carried away and did bad things in their own interest. If they committed a murder or started a war, there was no way to punish them. They were too powerful to argue with.

If you weren't fortunate enough to be born with medicine powers, then your parents usually helped you to try and get some. This is the second way of getting power. Long ago, people craved power and parents worked hard with their children to be good people and attract supernatural abilities.

Elders say you can't get medicine power if you are a bad person, if you have a dirty mind toward the opposite sex or animals, or if you brag and lie. You must be a good person and be capable of owning such powers. So, it looks like some greater power picks out only good people to receive medicine power. That's why many Dene believe it is the Creator who is its source.

As a result, many parents would tell their children to be good so that they might attract medicine power and help others, but it is not easy to get power in this way. Sometimes you work half your life and you get nothing. Sometimes, parents wanted their child to be

Boreal forest.

blessed with supernatural abilities so greatly that they isolated themselves. They lived apart in the bush so their offspring could be alone, maybe fasting and suffering for a few days, to attract power.

Some children accidentally got lost in the bush, or were left behind on purpose for a while when parents moved to a new camp; sometimes their power came to them while they were by themselves. The old people would say to children, "Go out to the bush and wait for something. Expect the unexpected." Maybe they would meet a talking animal or bird, or an old man or woman, from the spirit world who would give them their medicine power.

In the third way of getting medicine power, you inherit it from your parents or grandparents. This is by far the poorest way of getting it; if your powers come to you in this way they will be pretty weak because they have been almost used up by the owner before you. But, our ancestors wanted power so badly they would try anything. To make things even worse, often the person who got his abilities this way didn't live long because they aren't the rightful owners of the powers. They were not strong enough to bear it and it used them up. The power took a great deal of their energy. It was also easier for you to make a mistake with inherited power because you didn't know it too well; you could die from it going against you.

MEDICINE POWER—
A HELP AND A HINDRANCE

You can imagine, with so much medicine power available, there were lots of good and bad things happening when the world was new.

Wonderful things happened when medicine power was used in a good way. Some medicine people could talk to caribou hundreds of kilometres away and bring the herd close so hunters could feed their families. If someone had fish medicine, they could catch fish anywhere. With moose medicine, you could call the moose to come in and then you could kill them for meat.

Good shamans really helped everyone. They cared for the sick if they had the medicine for healing. Medicine people say everybody owns a spirit; it's attached to your body. If you go to see a shaman, they can see your spirit and they know what's wrong with you right away. If your spirit goes away, you die. You cannot live without your spirit. So if you are sick, the first thing a medicine person will do is check to make sure your spirit is within you.

Some medicine people can also trace your spirit back to a time when you lived on this earth before in another form. They can tell you of past incarnations, and the things you are supposed to learn in your present life.

When a shaman is making medicine, his or her spirit actually separates from the body. It looks as though the medicine person is just sitting or lying there, but his or her spirit is travelling to the spirit world to bring back help for the patient.

However, not all medicine people used their powers in a good way. Some owned too much medicine power and let it get the best of them, to the point where they saw themselves as being above everyone else.

These bad medicine people would put great fear in others and they were proud that they could make people cower before them. Some even bragged that they killed this or that person and then a war might break out, especially between different tribes who were trying to get even with a bad shaman's people.

Sometimes, a bad medicine person would make an individual suffer with sickness and, following this person's death, there would be a long investigation to find the perpetrator. Even if it became known who committed the murder, there was often nothing to be done if the bad shaman had strong powers over everyone else.

The only chance of getting rid of a bad medicine person was if a group of strong medicine people came together to confront the murderer. Then they would tell him, "Go away from here. Leave forever, or we will kill you right now." This was the only form of punishment my people had for this type of person.

PRAYER SONGS AND DRUM DANCES

Prayer was of the highest importance to my people. They used their drums and voices to sing or chant their requests and thanks to their Creator and to the spirits.

Even though our ancestors were scattered across a huge land and always moving, people gathered annually for drum dances. At these ceremonies, they prayed and gave offerings in gratitude for their lives and for the abundant provision of the Creator. After a good hunt or after survival of a long winter, a drum dance was often held.

My father would always light a fire after he shot a moose and place fat in it. He would talk to the fire a long time, thanking the Creator for the food and asking for continued good life for his family and people.

At the traditional tea dances which take place today, a feast of wild meat is prepared and, before everyone eats or drinks, offerings of food and tobacco are placed in the fire. This is called "feeding the fire." This great source of light and warmth represents the Creator. People place small, valuable things that they own in it as gifts while they talk to the fire, asking for help in their lives.

Elders stand up to pray and tell the people how the Creator made everything so they can live. They talk about higher powers that can help them if they live a clean life. They encourage people to always share and care for each other, for the animals, and for the earth.

If medicine people have any visions for the future or special messages for the people, they speak about them before the dancing begins. They share what they know about the spirit world in a way people will understand. They are also careful not to say too much to avoid breaking the taboo of silence they have to keep regarding their own powers.

As everyone dances around the fire to the beat of the drum, they pray for others and think good thoughts for their community. As you leave your footprints on the ground around the fire, you are building your trail to heaven. There is such a good feeling at drum dances; everyone is smiling and laughing and they remember they are all one family under the Creator. Their good thoughts make good things happen in the community.

The songs the drummers sing are special. They are ancient songs and many have been received in dreams. These chants fly up to the Creator and the spirits, asking for blessings for women and children, and for the hunters, or perhaps seeking guidance and strength to live a good life on this earth.

Medicine people enjoyed themselves at gatherings and cere-monies like the drum dance, where spirits were high and the people were happy to listen to their messages about living a good life. Some holy people had powers to influence people's minds and make them come to spiritual gatherings and listen to everything they said.

When you hit the drum, you are sounding the heartbeat of the people. Before Christianity came, the drum was our Bible. It opens up a channel to the Creator so our prayers are heard. As the old people say, if you sing your prayers, it is twice as powerful as if you just say them. Singing is powerful, and the repetition of Dene chants helps to centre your mind so you can be more in touch with the Creator.

When you are afraid, sometimes you sing to calm yourself. Prayer songs put you in a good frame of mind. You can sing out your gratitude to God or ask for blessings. The elders say animals and plants have their own songs and if we know how to sing them, they will help us.

View of the dance, Fort Rae, NWT 1937.

In 1931 a man called Yasuiley from Tulit'a (Fort Norman) began receiving one song from the spirits every week until, by the end of a year, he had fifty-two songs. He sang all the time, and Dene travelled kilometres to Fort Norman to hear his beautiful prayer songs that made them feel so connected with God.

After Yasuiley died in 1937 from tuberculosis, which had killed most of his Mountain Dene people, no one sang his songs anymore. They were almost forgotten until around 1975 when Tulit'a people began to revive them. I was a field worker sent to the community at that time to research land claims, and I used the tape recorder I had been issued to record a few of those wonderful old songs from the few elders left who still knew them.

I had a meeting with the Tulit'a elders and advised them to practice the songs as much as possible, to sing them at every drum dance feast and to teach them to the young people as well. Out of the fifty-two songs Yasuiley received, the people managed to keep only about twelve, but they still sing them today.

Some tea dance songs are so meaningful that when the drummers sing them, everyone gets up and dances. During prayer songs my people stand still and bow their heads in respect to the Creator. Prayer songs have been received in a dream by someone who has lived a good life. The visionary or prophet hands the songs down to the next generation and so some of them may be hundreds of years old.

Sometimes, someone who has died will send a song to a loved one in their dreams. Songs are sung to honour the holiness of life and to make us feel connected to our Creator and to each other.

WHY THERE IS NO MEDICINE POWER ANYMORE

░░░░░░░░░░░░

We have come from a time when every Dene owned a little or a great deal of medicine power, but today, in the 1900s, there are at most only ten medicine people recognized in all of Denendeh. What happened to extinguish our medicine power?

Some elders say medicine power is a loan from the Creator to help us live and that we don't need it now. We have grocery stores to feed us, and clothing stores to clothe us, and welfare cheques if we can't earn enough money to live. Medicine power was available when the survival of people was in question, when it meant the difference between life and death. In the modern world, we hardly ever have life and death survival situations, so the Creator took the powers back. We have churches for religion, the law protects us from criminals and we have our health care system to look after us when we get sick.

However, problems remain. For example, when the world was new there was no pollution. The water and air were clean. Humans, animals, birds, and fish enjoyed long and healthy lives. Now, Mother Earth is getting worn and old, and it seems she cannot take care of us the way she used to. Medicine powers are attached to the earth and they decrease and get weak just as Mother Earth does. She can't lend us her powers anymore like before. She is changed because of man's technology. Factory smoke that contains harmful chemicals goes into the air and drifts everywhere over the earth. It makes acid rain.

In some places, people can't eat the fish because of pollution in the water. On land, you can find wild animals and birds that are sick and diseased from maybe eating something that's been sprayed with pesticides and other chemicals. Medicine power was strong when the earth was clean and the people lived pure lives. Now the earth is polluted. You could say people's lives are contaminated, too.

The Creator gave us a good and powerful way to live. In our camps we used what the Creator gave us: we kept warm with fire, drank from the river, built sleds and traps from wood, ate roasted caribou and fish, and made our homes and clothes from animal hide and sinew. People died from accidents and starvation, they froze to death or were killed by enemies, but nevertheless there seemed to be a definite order and sacredness to life.

Grandparents and parents used Dene laws to help them teach children about male and female roles in life; girls prepared for motherhood and boys learned to be providers. Children were taught to treat the opposite sex with respect and that the creation of life was sacred.

In the medicine way, sex is looked upon as being sacred and special. You have to honour it and not talk about it or think anything bad about it. You become involved in sex only when you are old enough to get married.

Unfortunately, Europeans overlooked this important part of a child's education. Mission schools focused on religion and academic subjects, virtually ignoring emotional and social development. Priests and nuns taught children sex was bad, and they sometimes sexually abused children themselves because of their own unhealthy attitudes. The aftermath of this abuse still haunts us; incest within Dene families is a reality we are dealing with in our healing process.

Mainstream society, based on European values, has devalued the holiness of life and creation. Money and material goods are the trophies of living a good life. Pornographic magazines promote bad thinking about sex and strip bars are a common thing. We now have a sick way of looking at something that is, and must be considered as, sacred.

Today, we Dene give more importance to European culture than our own. Few live up to the medicine power laws that once ruled life. Many have become weakened and even dependent on alcohol, drugs, welfare, and television. Wildlife laws and the over-hunting of many animals make it hard for us to eat good, wild meat all of the time. We drink coffee and eat instant food full of chemicals; many children seem to live on pop, chips, and chocolate bars. Schoolteachers prepare our young ones for indoor jobs and the business world, and don't spend enough time on Dene culture and spirituality.

In Denendeh, the land is still wild and there are few roads and cities. Outside of S'ombak'e (Yellowknife), the land is mostly unde-veloped and its vastness and secrets still call to us. What place do the

Colville Lake camp.

things the Europeans taught us have here? Computer knowledge, for example, might be useful in downtown Toronto, but not in Denendeh. Harvesting and caring for the land is still most important.

A fight in 1926 between two shamans, who also forgot about Dene laws, helped to end the era of medicine power, our elders say. At that time, there were four medicine people recognized as the strongest in Denendeh. One of them lived in Aklavik, two in Tthedzeh Koe (Fort Wrigley) and one in Lutselk'e (Snowdrift).

It so happened that one of the strong medicine men was attending a feast in Tulit'a (Fort Norman) in the spring of 1926. A quarrel developed at the celebration; the shaman was accused of killing the son of another medicine man with his powers. The disagreement and bad feelings grew more and more intense until the men decided to kill each other.

The Tulit'a shaman was so angry that he said, "If I die I will take all of the medicine people with me." Three days later the strong medicine man died in the morning. In the evening of the same day, the other shaman died. People say that after their deaths, the 1928 flu epidemic hit Tulit'a and the rest of Denendeh.

That flu wiped out many people; and at their death so much knowledge and power passed away with them. People with lesser medicine tried to help stop the dying, but the power of the disease defeated them. A few medicine people may have survived, but that flu caused great loss for the Dene. We have never been the same since.

Prelude Lake, northeast of Yellowknife.

Chapter Four

YAMORIA'S GREAT
DENE MEDICINE LAWS

amoria is the great medicine man who came to change the lives of the Dene and encourage them to care for each other and establish equality. He travelled so much, and is so well known for his good deeds, that even Beaver tribes in northern British Columbia have stories about him. But where did he come from? Who sent him? One southern tribe in Denendeh says he was the Creator, or God, who lived among us and then went away.

The early missionaries who heard my ancestors tell stories of Yamoria said, "God sent this person to help you Dene to survive." Today, it's hard to believe how much Yamoria did to help people and the kind of miracles he made happen. Like a moosehide cape flowing from his shoulders, the legends of Yamoria sweep behind him across thousands of years.

Yamoria travelled around the world helping people who had problems with living, and he also gave them laws to live by at a time when there was much danger caused by bad shamans. Yamoria recognized how easy it was for a person with much power to use it the wrong way. He instructed parents and elders to teach his laws to children so they would be sure to live in peace. Elders gathered children every day, as soon as they could talk, to listen to stories about heroes and bad people of the past, and about the history of the world and human beings. The teachings were in the stories; the children were influenced to do good things like the good people in the legends and not to make the mistakes of the bad people.

These old Dene laws are still useful today. They should still be the first things we teach our young people. Even though they were given to us in a period much different from now, they are timeless. They are simple laws and if we follow them, we can still live a good life.

These are the laws that tradition teaches Yamoria first gave us:

DENE LAWS

1. SHARE WHAT YOU HAVE—This is the umbrella law; under it sit all the other laws. It was of absolute importance that people share what they had long ago, just for survival. Share all the big game you kill. Share fish if you catch more than you need for yourself and there are others who don't have any.

2. HELP EACH OTHER—Help elders cut their wood and other heavy work. Help sick people who are in need; get them firewood if they need it. Visit them and give them food. When you lose someone in death, share your sorrows with the relatives who are also affected by the loss. Help out widows as much as possible and take care of orphaned children.

3. LOVE EACH OTHER AS MUCH AS POSSIBLE—Treat each other as brother and sister, as though you are related. Help each other and don't harm anyone.

4. BE RESPECTFUL OF ELDERS AND EVERYTHING AROUND YOU—Don't run around when elders are eating. Sit down until they are finished.

5. SLEEP AT NIGHT AND WORK DURING THE DAY—Don't run around and laugh loudly when it gets dark. Everyone should sleep when darkness falls.

6. BE POLITE AND DON'T ARGUE WITH ANYONE—Don't harm anyone with your voice or your actions. Don't hurt anyone with your medicine power. Don't show your anger.

7. YOUNG GIRLS AND BOYS SHOULD BEHAVE RESPECTFULLY—Don't make fun of each other, especially in matters of sex. Don't make fun of older men and women. Be polite to each other.

8. PASS ON THE TEACHINGS—Elders are to tell stories about the past every day. In this way, young people learn to distinguish between good and unacceptable behaviour and when they are older, they will become the storytellers who will keep the circle of life going.

9. BE HAPPY AT ALL TIMES—The Creator has given you a great gift—Mother Earth. Take care of her and she will always give you food and shelter. Don't worry—just go about your work and make the best of everything. Don't judge people, find something good in everyone.

Just imagine how careful you would have had to be when strong medicine powers existed. Shamans who had power didn't talk about it so you had to be respectful around everyone; your neighbour could have many strong powers. He could hurt you if you made him angry. He could take away your spirit so your body became ill and you died. Then no one would even know what happened to you unless they got another medicine person to investigate your death to see how it was caused. This is why so many Dene laws have to do with respect and being polite.

Young children were also taught respect for nature and Mother Earth, what she provides for us to live and also about birds, animals, flowers and plants. Elders talked about the sun, stars, winds, clouds, fog, water, fish, and insects, and how the Creator made them for us to use. They told them about the conference human beings had with animals when it was decided the four-leggeds and winged ones would offer themselves for food if humans treated them with respect.

Elders would often tell children short stories about talking animals and birds so children could learn what these creatures think of human beings. The stories can explain the nature of each animal, why the Creator put them here, and what we can learn from them. Birds, for example, can teach us a lot about being happy because they are always chirping and singing.

As children became old enough to understand, they were taught the Dene laws and how to make a good life for themselves by watching and working with their parents.

Our ancestors believed the spirits were active at night so it was important to stay at home and go to sleep when the sun went down. When the sun came up, you got up too. No one stayed in bed during the day. To be strong and healthy it was important for people, especially the youth, to move around at all times. They didn't necessarily have to do hard work, just exercise that kept them active, like gathering and chopping wood, hauling water, hunting, paddling, and a lot of walking.

There are many other "common sense" Dene laws about work safety to prevent accidents and death. They offer advice like: be careful when you're hunting, fishing, or travelling in a small canoe; don't fight against nature, if there's a snowstorm, big waves on the lake, or heavy fog, don't venture out; learn how to swim; do not follow a caribou or moose onto a lake that's only been frozen two nights; be alert at all times and don't daydream or sleep while you're travelling in your sleigh or canoe; and don't pull a gun toward you by its barrel.

Other personal safety laws warn against eating too fast to prevent choking, and not to eat fat in hot weather.

Dene people learned these lessons and laws in body and mind. Even today elders don't usually sit still, they are always moving and they give away everything they have if they think someone needs it more than they. They grew up learning the laws of the land and it's hard to change them, even though everything around them seems different. Their sons, daughters, and grandchildren have become different people right before their eyes. Everyone speaks English now and they hardly ever hear the Dene languages.

Young people today are hard for elders to understand, who see how they behave toward each other and the ways their eating habits have changed. Very few are interested in the hunting and fishing culture; it's just too much work to try to make a living off the land.

Elders see life as a mixed-up affair now. It's hard for elders to change, but they do change a little. When you get elders and young people together to try to make a decision, especially a political one, it is very hard. Many elders would like to go back to life on the land, where everything seemed so simple. Still, it's also nice to have a few comforts that the modern world has brought.

We are paying a price for them, though. To get the money for these comforts, we work for companies that remove trees and minerals from the earth. That must be upsetting the balance of nature. I often wonder what, if anything, will be left here for our children's children?

Chapter Five

GREAT MEDICINE

PEOPLE

MALA JEEZON MEETS THE CREATURE GODENE

The Dene say huge monsters, and creatures called Godene, roamed the earth before the arrival of the great Yamoria.

Godene are part animal and part human. They resemble an enormous, overgrown man, but are much bigger and stronger. They have mighty medicine powers, even over most other shamans, and don't have respect for anything. They killed people and ate them. They had their own language and were always mumbling to themselves or to other Godene. Humans could not understand Godene, only medicine power people like Mala Jeezon could make sense of them.

Mala Jeezon was a strange person, as many medicine people are, because he had to act according to his powers. He travelled all over the world to help people, but he also liked to trick or scare them.

Once, when he was travelling in another country across the ocean, Mala Jeezon asked some people where he could go to meet a Godene. They showed him a place where they thought one might live.

Mala Jeezon hunted about for a while and finally he came upon a Godene's camp. No one was around and so he decided to play a trick on the shaggy creature. He spied a tree in front of the camp that would be just right for his prank. He made a hole in the tree trunk and then replaced the wood so it looked as it had before. Then he waited for Godene to return.

When Godene walked into his camp, he noticed Mala Jeezon right away. "What are you doing here?" he mumbled. 'I never see anybody here, you are the first who has come to see me. All the others are afraid of me because I eat them."

"I came to talk to you," said Mala Jeezon. "But before you kill me and eat me, I want you to challenge me. Do you see that tree over there? We'll try to hit it. The one who puts his fist right through it will be the boss."

Godene agreed to do this because Mala Jeezon was controlling his mind.

"You try first," Mala Jeezon instructed. Godene positioned himself in front of the tree and hit it with all his might. His hand went about two inches into the tree.

"Try again," said Mala Jeezon. Godene hit the tree and this time his fist went in about four inches.

"Let me try," Mala Jeezon said as he stepped up to the tree. Of course, he hit the tree in the place where he'd cut out the hole and his hand went right through. Godene looked at him in surprise.

"You see, I'm much stronger than you," Mala Jeezon told Godene. "I'm strong enough to kill you with my bare hand, so I'm your boss. Now you have to do what I say. Carry me back to my country and then I will give you orders on how you should live."

The two used their medicine powers to turn into spirits, and Mala Jeezon sat on Godene's back all the way back to North America. Halfway through the trip, Mala Jeezon rapped Godene on the head with a rock to get his attention.

"Ow! You hit me. That hurts," cried Godene.

"That was just a rock," Mala Jeezon told him and waved his fist in front of Godene's eyes. "If I hit you with this you wouldn't be alive, so stop complaining!"

Godene kept quiet and soon they arrived back in North America.

"I'll give you orders on how you are to live, and you have to obey me from now on," Mala Jeezon told Godene once they had landed. "If you don't listen to me, I'll look for you and kill you.

Not only you but all the Godene in this country will disappear. I want you to get busy and tell all your friends what I say. From now on don't kill any more human beings for food. Hunt only animals as we do, to eat. You can trying fishing, too. You are smart enough to do that. So go now, go wherever you want to, but remember what I said to you."

From that time on Godene stopped killing human beings, thanks to Mala Jeezon.

THE BIRTH OF YAMORIA
AND HIS BROTHER YAMOGA

Long ago, there was a family living on the land. The husband, wife, and their young daughter visited their fishnets and checked their rabbit snares every day for food. The girl had her own set of snares and she often walked by herself to see if she'd caught anything.

One night she was coming home and was disturbed by a sound. There was no wind, but she noticed that a small tree near her kept moving back and forth. She was surprised to hear the little tree making so much noise. Then she realized the sounds she heard were the cries of a baby. She became frightened and ran all the way home.

Out of breath, she finally reached her tent. "What's the matter?" her mother asked her. As her daughter described how the small tree had moved back and forth while the other trees stood still and then she'd heard the sound of a baby crying, her mother nodded.

"Maybe medicine powers want to reach you," she told her daughter. "Go to that snare as usual at the same time tomorrow and when you get to the spot near that tree, think very strongly to yourself. Think 'I want to hear the baby cry again.' If the baby cries, say to yourself 'Please, let me see something.' If this thing happens again and if you are supposed to receive medicine powers, maybe something will happen."

That night the daughter could hardly sleep as she thought about the baby crying. The next day, towards evening, she came to the small tree that had moved back and forth.

"I want to hear the baby cry. I want to hear the baby cry," she thought to herself, over and over. After a little while, the small tree started to move again, back and forth—and then she heard the baby cry again. The baby must be right inside the tree!

"Please let me see the baby," she thought, with all her heart. The tree started to shake and pretty soon it fell over; its roots were exposed, and a muddy hole appeared where it had once stood.

Two babies lay in the mud, crying harder than ever! The girl jumped into the hole and scooped the babies up, wrapping them in her coat. She hurried home.

When her mother saw the babies, she knew they were special. She and her daughter wrapped the babies in warm hides and fed them rabbit broth and brains. They treated them well. The babies grew fast and became the great medicine people, Yamoria and his brother Yamoga. They appeared on this earth without being born of a woman.

When the boys were about six years old, the family they lived with went moose hunting. Everyone went along, including the family's grandfather, who was losing his mind a bit.

When the family saw fresh moose tracks, they took off on the hunt, leaving Yamoria and Yamoga with the old grandfather, camped near a lake. The old man liked the boys because they were special and he let them play on the lakeshore for a long time.

When it was getting close to bedtime, the grandfather shouted for the boys to come to bed. When they came into the tent he told them how much his head hurt.

"I've got lice in my hair," he told them. "Kneel down close to my head and if you find lice, pick them out and throw them in the fire."

The children knelt down by the old man's head and began to pick out lice and throw them into the fire. It was a lot of fun for them and they laughed loudly. But the old man was so deaf he didn't even hear them; he fell fast asleep.

Pretty soon, Yamoria found a hole in the old man's skull. He felt further with his fingers and discovered the brain, soft and squishy. The kids were surprised to find the hole and became curious about what would happen if they put something into it.

"I will throw a hot rock from the fire in there," Yamoria told Yamoga. Yamoga held the old man's hair back while Yamoria threw the rock in.

The old man stretched suddenly and jerked, then he shook violently. The boys laughed and laughed at the old man, until finally he lay dead on the ground. The boys thought their grandfather had fallen asleep again so they went back outside to play.

Soon the hunters came back and the boys told them about the hole they'd found and what they had done. The family was sad but realized the children had not meant to kill their grandfather.

YAMORIA AND YAMOGA
BECOME GREAT MEDICINE PEOPLE

These two brothers had strong medicine powers and did a lot to help the Dene. They had powers for everything. They had strong powers of authority to control people's minds. They tried to bring people together and urged them to help, share, and work with each other. They came to earth during a dangerous time, when many evil people harmed others with strong medicine and huge animals scared everyone.

Yamoria became more famous than his brother for helping people, while Yamoga became more widely known as a warrior who was always fighting. The brothers travelled across the North to talk to groups of Dene wherever they could. But the land was so big and the people so scattered, it was impossible to meet everyone. The brothers decided to split up so they could reach more people and teach them how to live in a good way.

Yamoga travelled in the Deh Cho (Mackenzie River) Mountain Range, along the Yukon border. Storytellers east of the mountains have few stories about his life; however, they have many about his brother Yamoria.

YAMORIA TRAVELS AMONGST THE DENE

Yamoria started to travel and teach people when he was very young. His strong powers told him he would live a long life and so he used his time on earth to confront people about their wrongdoing and encourage them to respect and love each other. He feared no one.

Yamoria didn't act like a human being. For example, he had powers for spirit travel. He could be standing in one place and then disappear, rematerializing hundreds of kilometres away a minute later. To do this he would transform himself into spirit to move through space and time, and then transform back into a human being when he got to the place he wanted to go. He covered a huge area in his lifetime. People talk about him from what is now Fort St. John, British Columbia, to northern Alberta and all the way to the Deh Cho Delta on the Beaufort Sea.

When Yamoria met with a group of Dene he would say, "I come to help you. If you have problems with bad medicine people or dangerous animals, tell me. I want to change your life so that you can work together and be happy."

Yamoria destroyed the giant bats, beaver, monsters, and dinosaurs that ate people by bringing a great sickness that killed them one by one. And when it came to dealing with bad medicine people, Yamoria was also merciless. When he first started to visit people to help them, no one knew exactly how powerful he was and why he had no fear, especially from evil shamans whom no one else dared confront. He would first try to talk some sense into them and if they didn't listen, he would destroy them.

After Yamoria was forced to kill a troublesome medicine

person, he established his authority with the Dene. "I killed this bad shaman," he would tell the crowd. "He deserved it!" Then he would look at those who had medicine power and tell them, "Do not harm anyone. If you do, I will end your life, too. When I leave your area, I will have my spiritual powers check up on you medicine people. If you hurt someone, I will know about it and I will kill you! Look what I did to that man yesterday. He thought he was strong, but he was not!"

Yamoria made the people understand that medicine power was given to the people by the Creator to help them, not to harm others with. They should always share the gains that came of owning medicine power with each other.

Yamoria sounds like a mean person, but he had taken on a very dangerous mission in confronting powerful medicine people who had no fear or respect for anyone or anything. He was a good man, but he used his powers to kill if he had to. Yamoria met many violent people in his travels and death was the only way to handle them. It wasn't easy for Yamoria to go into communities as a stranger and have to confront and perhaps kill someone, but he did it so human beings could have a better life.

Soon the whole North country knew about Yamoria's great medicine powers and that he could overrule anyone. Most medicine people began to behave better and life became safer, more peaceful. The strong shamans stuck to themselves and didn't bother anyone, unless they were bothered.

Yamoria accomplished a difficult mission. He dealt with the spiritual or medicine power world in which you can't see or know what's going on unless you have medicine powers to cover everything.

Yamoria also gave the Dene medicine laws to live by. He called meetings wherever he went and told them, "I want elders and parents to teach their children as soon as they start to talk. I want the elders to tell stories of the past, every day, and talk about good people and bad people. Talk about the mistakes they have made and how people suffered from it. Try to prevent these mistakes from happening again. I want you to work together and share everything you have. Or, you can elect a person to be your leader. Pick a strong person. A respected leader has to be a strong medicine man, so they will know what is going on if there is a problem."

Yamoria gave parents laws to teach their children. "Share everything, visit the sick and help them. If people die, try to help those left behind. Love each other, don't make anyone angry by what you say or do. Be polite to each other. Respect everyone, especially strangers. Be careful who you talk to because there are a lot of bad medicine people around and you never know who they are." He said this because of the dangerous medicine time he lived in.

Yamoria wanted people to live softly on the earth and to have a good system to live by. He helped the Dene to communicate better and encouraged elders to teach their families about planning for the future and respecting Mother Earth.

The elders spoke about spirituality and praying with the drum. They also showed people how to feed the fire in honour of the spirit world. Strong medicine people began to share the knowledge they had previously kept secret. They spoke of a high power in the spirit world that looks down upon the earth.

"We can pray and ask favours if we are good people, and the Creator may listen to us," they told the Dene. The people began to pray with the drum and create ceremonies to honour the spirit world. They learned it was this higher power that gave out medicine powers to help people.

It took a long time, but eventually people stopped their wicked ways and lived cleaner lives. Yamoria got the Dene started on self-education and self-government. Soon, all elders saw themselves as teachers and told stories every day to pass on the laws that Yamoria gave them. All children grew up with these laws and never forgot them. The people gathered often to tell stories, sing, beat the drum, and pray together.

YAMORIA AND THE BAD MEDICINE WOMAN

There was once a bad medicine woman who lived on the north end of Jacho (Great Slave Lake). She made trouble for the people who lived near her and to those who had to travel past her, on their way into the Barren Lands to hunt caribou. Several people had lost their lives because of her.

The people were afraid of this powerful woman. They wished they could talk to Yamoria about her. Yamoria was always travelling from camp to camp, listening to people complain about bad medicine people in their settlement who were too strong for their own good, and who scared everyone.

A group from the north end of Tucho travelled to see if Yamoria could help them with this troublesome woman. Yamoria investigated the problem spiritually and found out the woman had unusually strong medicine power. Then he told the group he would travel with them to see the woman.

When he arrived near her home, where she lived alone, he had no problem finding her. She had no idea that this was the great Yamoria and that he had already investigated how much medicine power she owned.

"You'd better behave better from now on," Yamoria told her. "Don't harm anyone anymore, or I will punish you."

Since this woman had such strong powers she wasn't afraid

of anyone and she made no effort to control her temper.

"Who are you to tell me what to do?" she shouted at Yamoria.

Yamoria calmly repeated that she shouldn't harm anyone again or she would be sorry for her actions.

The woman began to flirt and behave seductively toward Yamoria, attempting to lure him into her place. Yamoria suspected this was her usual game—attracting men into her home and then killing them.

So Yamoria ignored her and pretended to walk away. He circled her dwelling to investigate her more closely, but the woman followed him. Yamoria circled her place two more times and noticed the woman was still with him. On the third round, Yamoria walked into a rock cliff and the woman followed him. He came out of the rock a little farther on but the woman stayed inside.

The woman is still caught in the cliff rock. When she perished, all of her power became available to Dene people. Today people still go to the landmark to ask for favours and good luck.

Storytellers say when people placed offerings along the cliff long ago, the payment would be gone by the next day—accepted by the woman inside.

People continue to have a strong belief in the Woman-In-The-Rock's powers and leave her offerings, though they don't disappear as they once did.

YAMORIA GETS FOOLED BY THE ANIMALS

When the world was new a lot of strange things happened. If you were out walking on the land and met someone you didn't know, you never quite knew who they were. Sometimes they weren't human beings at all, but animals instead. Animals could slip into different bodies so easily, they could fool anyone.

Even Yamoria got fooled by animals. He was travelling in the north country when he met a woman who lived by herself. "She's very nice looking," he thought to himself, noticing that she also seemed to have a lot of food and enough hides to live well.

While the woman was cooking, she and Yamoria talked. The woman began to tease him. "What's a nice looking man like you doing wandering in the bush all by yourself?" she asked. Then she laughed at him and he laughed too.

After they finished eating, the woman suggested they live together as a couple and Yamoria agreed.

Yamoria hunted often and the woman ordered him to act in a certain way when he was out on the land.

"If you have to cross a creek, please cut a willow and place it across the stream, and then cross. Don't forget to do this. It's important to me," she told him. Yamoria didn't understand why she wanted him to do this, but he obeyed her.

After they had lived together for a long time, one day Yamoria was in the bush far from home and, noticing it was getting dark, hurried to return. He came upon a creek and, in his hastiness, decided it wouldn't hurt just this once not to place the willow across it first.

When he arrived home he found his wife gone. That

evening, he suspected the woman might be up to something and used his powers to investigate her closely. Yamoria found out the woman was actually a beaver. He began to feel angry and a bit foolish that he had been tricked into caring about a woman who was actually a beaver. He decided to find out more about the beaver-woman.

He traced her disappearance to a big lake which today is called Lac La Mort. At the far end of the lake, a family of giant beaver lived well by killing and eating the Dene who ventured into this area known as ?Weecho Showae (Giant Lands). The beaver were building a dam on this lake and weren't quite finished before Yamoria chased them out. Today the dam looks like a narrow strip of land in the water about four miles long with a small opening in the middle.

Yamoria chased the beaver family down the French Channel in front of where Behcho Ko (Fort Rae) now stands. It was here the beaver stopped to eat and the Dene living nearby became frightened by the gnawing sounds the huge animals were making.

Yamoria caught up with them there and kept chasing the beaver toward Tucho (Great Slave Lake) and across it, until finally he herded them down Deh Cho.

Years later, he caught up with the Giant Beaver again. They were living at Great Bear Lake, and there he took more drastic action. This time, he chased them up Deh Cho toward the place where Tulit'a (Fort Norman) now stands. Here, he killed three of them, skinned them, and tacked the hides to Great Bear Rock. You can still see the three huge, oval-shaped outlines of the beaver pelts there today. It is a well-known Dene landmark.

ECHSONE SAVES HIS FAMILY

This legend is thousands of years old, from when the world was new. It's about Echsone, who made history because he used his great powers to help people who were having a hard time. He knew when someone was having a problem; if that person mentioned his name, he would go to help them.

Echsone always carried a bag of dried animal muscle. When he received a signal that someone needed him he would throw a piece of muscle into the fire. When it melted into a ball, he would disappear and then reappear where he wanted to be.

Echsone's four brothers, sister, and mother had followed a caribou herd hunting for food and ended up living amongst strangers in an unfamiliar land. Unfortunately, Echsone's brothers had angered this tribe; perhaps they had been impolite or hadn't followed the tribe's culture. Now, they were sentenced to die.

Echsone's brothers and sister had been ordered to dance their last dance on earth in preparation for death, while their widowed mother sat in a lodge and cried for her children.

"I wish my son Echsone was here, he would know what to do," she moaned.

Hundreds of miles away, Echsone stood up in his tipi. "Somebody is in trouble. I have to go to them," he told his wife, digging for his bag. Throwing dried animal muscle into the fire, he pronounced his medicine words and was gone. His wife and neighbour were used to Echsone's medicine and knew he would be back.

Echsone entered his mother's lodge and asked why she was crying.

"Oh Echsone, these people are going to kill us all! They are making us dance our last dance!" she sobbed.

"I'll go and do what I can. You stay here and wait," Echsone answered.

He walked to where his brothers and sister were dancing before a crowd of people. Echsone joined them in their circle. Right away the people recognized him. He was known all over the country as a strong medicine man to be feared. The dancing stopped and Echsone faced the crowd.

"If you want to kill people, try me! Come on, kill me!" he shouted. The crowd backed away in terror.

"Pack up your things and we'll start travelling home," Echsone angrily told his brothers. "You boys can't handle yourselves among strangers. You're too mouthy. You have to talk and act according to Dene law in order to get along better with people, especially strangers. We'll go home. I'll travel with you."

Echsone's family packed and left unharmed.

MEDICINE POWER WOMAN

One cold winter, two sisters named Jumping Marten and White Flower were travelling on the land with their husbands searching for food. The women towed a caribou leg-hide "toboggan" or bag behind them, filled with their meagre possessions, while the men went ahead, searching for game.

Two men who were enemies of the young couples came across the husbands' tracks and decided to make trouble. They built a barricade from fallen trees across the husbands' path to create a detour for the women they knew would be coming behind. The women hardly noticed the barricade and unwittingly followed the new path, which led them right into their enemy's camp.

As the sisters approached, Jumping Marten, the oldest of the two, realized they'd been tricked as soon as she heard the strange language the men were speaking. But it was too late. The two men jumped up and began to hit the women and sexually abuse them. They made the sisters cook the only two fish they had with them, greedily devouring the food in front of the women without sharing a bite.

In the women's toboggan the men found two moccasin cutouts ready to be sewn. They ordered the women to each sew one of the moccasins for them. In the dark of night, the two sisters tried to make holes with an awl in the moosehide, and push lengths of sinew through them to sew the shoes together, but it was difficult work. The men slapped the women and yelled at them to work quicker.

Across the fire, Jumping Marten could hear her sister crying. She felt sorry for little White Flower and made up her mind to do something about their situation. She exposed her bare leg to the cold so the tiny holes in the moosehide would show up better against the whiteness of her skin, and quickly finished sewing the moccasin. Then Jumping Marten finished sewing the moccasin her sister was working on as well.

After the men and her sister fell asleep, Jumping Marten began to think about ways of escaping from the men, and the subject of medicine power came into her mind. She concentrated on her life before birth and realized she had lived one life before this present one. She remembered a significant event that had occurred just prior to her second birth.

An old man and woman had visited her to give her medicine power and advice on how to use it. The old woman introduced herself as Eehsine Unla and said, "Anytime you want to make medicine power, think hard and call me. I will come to help you. You are a woman and will grow up soon. You will have the choice to use sex in a good way to make children, or to use it only for pleasure. If you have sex with someone, you will have the power to control their mind and make their life miserable if you want to."

Then the old man introduced himself as Eehsie Choh and said, "I give to you owl medicine and you can use it to help people if you want. There are five different kinds of owls, from very smart to very stupid. You can use their medicine for many different purposes."

So now Jumping Marten called upon Eehsine Unla and Eehsie Choh to help her. They materialized before her eyes and asked how they could help her. She told the old man and woman how the men had abused them and how she wanted to get away from them.

"We could kill them for you right now," said Eehsine Unla. "Or, since they have had sex with you, you can control their minds."

"Yes, with your owl medicine you can make them crazy," added Eehsie Choh. "Their minds will be taken over by the crazy owl and they won't even know you're here. They won't even know how to care for themselves in this cold weather."

Jumping Marten decided to have the men lose their minds. Then, before the old man and woman disappeared, she memorized the medicine words they gave her so she could work her medicine power on her own in the future.

Jumping Marten roused White Flower and told her to pack their toboggan. As they were leaving, Jumping Marten kicked both her enemies in the stomach and told them to get up. The men sat up, and Jumping Marten looked into their vacant eyes, laughing at their craziness. She knew they would suffer in the cold and probably die from their inability to help themselves.

Jumping Marten became a famous medicine woman, using her mind control, owl, and sexual attraction powers to help women who came to her when they suffered abuse from men. If a woman wanted to attract a certain special man to herself, Jumping Marten would use her sexual attraction medicine to get the couple together.

In her long life, Jumping Marten killed two medicine men who possessed powers similar to hers, but who could not override her stronger female power. Even though she was considered to be dangerous by many, she helped many people heal from all kinds of sickness and used her medicine to confront people who were abusing their power.

EDZO OVERPOWERS THE GREAT ENEMY

By the early 1800s, the Chipewyan nation was the largest in Denendeh. Their nation was strung across the North, from what today is called Fort Churchill, Hudson Bay, west to the Rocky Mountains, about 3,200 kilometres away. They followed the caribou up into the Barren Lands and travelled as far as Coppermine and the Yukon River, to trade.

The Chipewyan were powerful shamans and not afraid of anyone. Smaller tribes were terrified of them. This powerful tribe controlled the northward movement of the early fur traders by obtaining guns, knives, axes, and other tools and keeping them away from other tribes. They established themselves as middlemen in the fur trade.

Edzo belonged to the Dogrib Nation, which lived west of

where S'ombak'e (Yellowknife) is today, and farther north toward Sahtu (Great Bear Lake), Itseretue (Hottah Lake) and Tsoti (Lac La Martre). He was still a young medicine man when a group of his people decided to travel about 1,200 kilometres across Deh Cho to the Shih Kaedenila (Rocky Mountains) to see if they could trade for the new European goods they had heard so much about. They travelled all summer, through swamps, muskeg, and swarms of mosquitoes. It was winter when they reached the mountain country.

Along the way, Slavey hunters directed them southward, toward where Fort St. John stands today. This is where they could trade fur, drymeat and moosehides for axes, guns, and knives.

The Dogrib were heading into Chipewyan territory and sent two spies out to see if it was safe to proceed. These two never came back. Much later, they sent two more spies, and when they also failed to return they sent two more, whom they never saw again either.

By this time the Dogrib had spent two years in the Rocky Mountains, hunting big game along the way. They finally decided to send two more spies to see what had happened to their friends, but when they also failed to return, they decided on a new tactic.

A group of ten of their strongest warriors, plus Edzo and Kozieda, another medicine man, went to see what had happened to the eight lost men. On the way into Chipewyan lands they learned from Slavey travellers that their people had been killed by the Chipewyan.

Meanwhile, Dogrib leader Edzo received a "moccasin tele-graph" (word of mouth) message from the renowned Chipewyan Chief Ebecho."You are afraid of me and so you hide yourself in the mountains," Ebecho challenged Edzo. Edzo and his group decided to avenge the deaths of their friends and so they eventually found their way into the Chipewyan camp in the upper Peace River country.

It didn't take long for a confrontation to occur. The Dogrib angered the Chipewyan with their accusations of murder. An argument followed and Kozieda jumped up and cut the ear off one of the Chipewyan medicine men with his stone axe. Edzo yelled at his group to leave quickly before the situation became more violent, and the group fled home to their wives and children back in the mountains.

After two years of travel to trade for modern tools, the Dogrib fled empty handed back to Itseretue. Arriving home months later, they learned the Dogrib were in great danger because the Chipewyan there had been losing men and were accusing the Dogrib of killing them. Edzo's people could not hunt caribou in the Barren Lands for fear of meeting the Chipewyan seeking vengeance.

Edzo assured the people he would protect them with his powers and took small parties into the Barren Lands to hunt. On their way back with caribou meat, they met a small Chipewyan group from Great Slave Lake who were friendly because their leader, Katewee, was Edzo's brother-in-law. From this group, Edzo learned the Chipewyan were enraged because several of their hunters had disappeared and the Dogrib were being blamed for killing them.

Edzo sent word to Katewee that he would visit him in a week to plan a meeting with the Chipewyan. Back in his own camp, he tried to group his people together to get their support in making peace with the Chipewyan, but the people were afraid. Edzo went to other Dogrib camps, gathering elders and medicine men to influence his people to stand up to the Chipewyan.

As he stood before his people with the visitors he had gathered, Edzo knew he had to spur them into action.

"We are worthy people. We can't let things get away on us. If we don't do anything now, we might have war ahead of us. I want to meet the Chipewyan leader Akaitcho," he shouted. "Yes, he is a powerful medicine man and the leader of the largest tribe in the country, but we can't let the Chipewyan, no matter how powerful they are, give us a hard time. We have to protect our people, not only with strong words and shouting. The Chipewyan keep many things from us. They stand between us and the traders who could give us guns to fight with."

The people were afraid of Edzo and did not say a word, so Edzo continued.

"I am not afraid to face Akaitcho alone. Yes, he is a great medicine man, but there are so many kinds of power I might be able to find a loophole and override him. I have powers for out-talking anyone. That's why I always speak loudly and people are afraid of me. If Akaitcho can't out-talk me, then I might be able to overcome him.

"But, there is one thing. The Chipewyan are very strong medicine people and I will be facing so many of them. I need assistance from you, my own people. Then I will be stronger."

Edzo talked loud and long to his people, but in the end he was only able to persuade two medicine men and a fourteen-year-old boy to go with him.

These people set out to face the large Chipewyan tribe to make peace. They settled at the end of the lake Katewee was camped on, some distance still from the main enemy camp. Edzo first made medicine to find out if he and his people would be alive to see the next day, then he slipped away in the evening darkness to spy on Akaitcho.

As he crouched in the bush along a trail to the lake, an elderly woman walked by with her water container. Edzo recognized her as his sister. He whistled at her and when she turned around, she saw who it was and hurried toward him. The two hugged and then Edzo's sister led him to her tent where she told him of Chipewyan plans.

"Right this minute there's a meeting in Akaitcho's tent. They want to kill all Dogrib, because they blame them for the death of the hunters. You are here at a bad time. The best I can do is have my husband come to talk to you."

Later that night, Katewee came from Akaitcho's meeting to find his wife hiding Edzo. Even though Katewee tried to talk his brother-in-law out of taking action against Akaitcho, Edzo was stubborn.

"There are only four of us. We need your help. Tomorrow morning, take a small group of men—some of your warriors and three of Akaitcho's hunters and one of his runners. Pretend you're looking around. Tell your warriors to make it look like you came upon our camp by accident."

Katewee agreed to the plan and Edzo snuck back to his small camp. He made medicine long into the night to see how he could overpower Akaitcho and found that, yes, he could use his voice to out-talk him. Edzo shouted at one of his men, who had medicine for mind-control, to work beside him.

"There's no time to lose. We must get ready. Akaitcho's men will be here soon," Edzo said.

Edzo's partner began to make his medicine. He took a beaverhide from his bag and heated it over the fire until it became soft. He spread it in front of him, speaking medicine words and waving his hands over it for a long time. Finally, he sat on it and spoke to his friends. "I have put all of the Chipewyan minds into this beaverhide and I will control their minds as long as I sit on this hide. Whatever I think, our enemies will think. When I think peace, they will think peace. So, you don't have to be afraid. They won't think of fighting you."

Four canoes glided along the shoreline at noon the next day. Three of them belonged to Katewee's people and one belonged to Akaitcho's.

When they came close to Edzo's camp, Akaitcho's runner back-paddled his canoe and shouted he had to go back to his camp to get his knife. As he yelled the news of the Dogrib's location from his canoe, the Chipewyan grabbed their guns, bows, arrows, clubs, and knives, surging forward to meet their despised enemy.

Akaitcho's warriors dared not take action before their leader arrived. They watched as Akaitcho reached the shore and stepped out of his canoe. There the four Dogrib sat, with Edzo lying face down on the sand, not even looking at Akaitcho's men.

"Ah, I have wanted to do this for a long time," Akaitcho snarled, poking his big knife into Edzo's side. "I am in a mood to kill and you'll be the first one!"

Still Edzo did not turn to look at his enemy.

"We have been losing men all across the country and you are responsible. This has to stop," Akaitcho said, uncomfortable to be addressing a great leader in this way. He couldn't just stab him in the back. They all thought Edzo was so scared he couldn't move or utter a word.

"It's no good for two groups to fight each other all the time. We should have peace now," Akaitcho continued, as his warriors crouched with their knives, ready to kill the Dogrib. But their leader kept talking, sometimes about war, sometimes about peace.

Finally, Edzo turned toward Akaitcho. His appearance had changed. His face was sweaty, dark and ugly. His hair swept upwards, and dark fluid ran from his mouth.

"So you want peace. I am not quite ready to talk peace with you. I also have wanted to kill you for a long time," roared Edzo, as thunder boomed and a strong wind bent the willows and spruce to the ground.

The Chipewyan were frightened. They knew strong medicine people could kill others using water, wind, snow, sun, or rain.

"You blame us Dogrib for your problems. You cause us problems, too. We have lost many hunters to you. You have killed them. You prevent us from seeing the white traders. You don't own them, yet you prevent us from going to them to trade fur."

Edzo stood to face Akaitcho; in his anger he looked even bigger than he actually was. "If you want war, we will have war," he snarled, pointing his finger at his enemy.

Akaitcho suddenly cowered, putting his hand out. "My friend, don't talk like that. I don't want to fight. I want peace. We will forget about some things that we have against each other. We will speak only of peace arrangements."

The two leaders spoke together for a long time. Then Akaitcho turned to address his warriors. "From now on there will be no war talk. Any one of my people who kills a Dogrib will be punished by me. I will settle all problems myself. We will treat the Dogrib as brothers, from now on. We will help them to travel and will share what we have. We will let them see the white traders in our area. We want to live in peace," he exclaimed.

Edzo spoke next, his voice ringing out across the water. "This peace must last forever amongst us. These white traders, they are not honest people, they want too much from us. They take many furs and give back only a little. We will become poor working for them and providing ourselves with food. We have to travel so far to get fur and far again when we go to trade.

"I have looked into the future. These white traders are not the big boss. More white people will come and they will say they are the boss of everything and push us around. They will say 'this land is ours' and make laws of their own and make us obey them. And they have enough guns to kill us all if they want to.

"My people, what I say here is the truth. It is my purpose to look ahead. The white people will give us many more problems in the future. That time will not be long from now, so it is foolish to fight amongst ourselves for revenge. We must stay together and help each other to be strong. I want peace forever. Wherever I travel I will repeat this, to my own people. No disputes, even if both sides lose hunters. We will not blame each other and talk violent. I repeat, I want peace forever."

Akaitcho stood close to Edzo and shook his hand. "Enough talking here my friend, come to my tent and we will have a great feast and dance. We will show our people we mean what we say. We will repeat our peace proclamation at the feast. Come now!"

Edzo gladly agreed and he and his men rode to the huge Chipewyan camp. Everywhere, people could not believe their eyes. The two leaders walked together. Akaitcho ordered a feast be prepared of the best food they had. It was quickly prepared and eaten, and then the leaders explained the peace arrangement to the people once more.

Some were afraid many individuals were still "awetii," killers who strike others down without feeling, but their leaders talked of peace until their fears were calmed. A drum dance followed the meal and it lasted for three days and nights. One of Edzo's men had animal and bird dancing medicine powers and when he used them, the people were drawn as if by a magnet to the dance ring. The ground beneath them was torn to pieces and the dance circle can still be seen to this day.

The two great tribes laid down their weapons in peace. Edzo played an important role in confronting the Chipewyan, but without his fellow shaman who "sat" on people's minds to control them, there might have been violence on that day so long ago. The Dogrib and Chipewyan nations could have been destroyed, but they have lived in peace ever since.

EZEETAN MAKES PEACE

Told by Edward Blondin, Deline (Fort Franklin)

On a spring morning, while a group of Gwich'in fished on the banks of Deh Cho, one of the many wars they fought with the Inuit began.

Men and women had been busily catching and drying fish on both sides of the river, but then one morning one group noticed no smoke coming from the other's fires. Since Inuit attacks were common, two young warriors set out right away to see what was wrong. They returned crying and sobbing about the blood and death they had seen on the other side. In the night, the Inuit—who were silent and stealthy warriors who had not yet acquired guns— had crept into the camp and killed everyone with knives and axes.

Amidst much weeping and wailing, a voice rang out. It was the shaman Ezeetan, who had lost his relatives in the massacre, shouting, "Let's do something about this madness. It is too late to cry. Let the old ones deal with the bodies and burn the clothing, I will take the young men and find our enemy."

He returned to his home camp with the warriors and made medicine for the cold and the north wind to come. He told his men to pack for winter and they jumped in their canoes, and followed the Inuit toward the Arctic ocean.

The temperature dropped and ice started to form on the shore. They paddled through blowing snow all day and night, reaching the ocean early the next morning. Behind a grove of willow they saw the smoke of an Inuit camp.

Ezeetan cried out, "My name is Ezeetan. You have killed our relatives and now we come to kill you!" Taken by surprise, the

Inuit had no time to react and all were killed easily by Gwich'in guns and bows and arrows, except for one man. Ezeetan told him, "I have saved your life. Go home and tell your people that I will be waiting for them next summer if they want to fight again."

During the winter, Ezeetan married. Now that it was spring, he and his wife took a small canoe and travelled downriver to hunt ducks. After two days and one night, they had killed as many ducks as they could pack. Exhausted, Ezeetan told his wife he wanted to rest in the tall grass along the river. Since he was always alert for the return of the Inuit, he was careful not to leave tracks in the wet mud beside the water.

He would have been restless had he known that, just up the river, the Inuit had returned in their kayaks and wiped out two Gwich'in camps. While one Inuit group returned home, seventeen more kayaks continued downriver, checking the shoreline for tracks and looking for fish nets or signs in the water showing that Gwich'in had passed by. When one of the Inuit noticed a small mark in the mud made by Ezeetan's paddle, he climbed out of his kayak to investigate.

"Stay here. I'll go and check the area," the lead warrior told his men. Up on the bank he found Ezeetan's canoe hidden in the willows. When a second kayak arrived, the four Inuit crept farther into the bush, sniffing for smoke.

In the grass, Ezeetan and his wife slept soundly. When the Inuit attacked, Ezeetan woke up and worked his medicine powers to help him move quickly. He cracked the heads of the two Inuit holding him and then stabbed the two who were holding his wife. They ran for their canoe and waited in the grass for more Inuit to arrive. When two more kayaks came down the river, Ezeetan shot four more Inuit.

"No more seem to be coming," Ezeetan told his wife and so they began to paddle home. Soon, they heard their people singing up the river and Ezeetan feared the worst.

"We have been away too long. The Inuit have struck hard. There will be time to mourn your family's death, but for now we have to work hard to make amends," Ezeetan told his wife. "The enemy have no guns but I still have lots of powder and bullets. We will go to meet the Inuit in the middle of the Deh Cho."

Sure enough, they met twelve kayaks in the middle of the huge river and Ezeetan opened fire on them. His bullets killed many men and many more were drowned after he shot their vessels full of holes. Once more, the great shaman saved the life of one man and told him, "Don't forget, my name is Ezeetan and I will be waiting for your people if they want to fight some more."

Ezeetan and his wife returned home to mourn with their people over the death of their people. Following the death rituals, everyone moved far up the river to other Gwich'in camps.

The following summer, Inuit kayaks again travelled upriver, but this time they were filled with elders carrying gifts for Ezeetan. When they found him, they asked for peace between their nations. Wanting the killing to stop, they begged the medicine man for his cooperation and blessing.

Ezeetan, though a powerful shaman who feared no one, had shed too many tears for relatives lost in bloody wars, and so he gladly accepted the gifts and agreed to stop the fighting. The Inuit peace party paddled homeward, knowing they no longer had to fear the Gwich'in.

BLONDIN WANTS HIS POWERS REMOVED

Before the flu epidemic hit Denendeh in the 1920s, there were several great medicine people in Denendeh. Edward Blondin, my great-grandfather from Aklavik, was one.

He was born somewhere around 1835 and died in 1926. His parents were Gwich'in but both died when he was born. He was adopted by a French trapper and occasional trader named Blondin, which is how he got his European name.

Blondin had great medicine powers but he didn't appreciate them. Earlier I mentioned that medicine people were often strange and had to live differently from others according to the rules set for them by their powers. Blondin was young and didn't want to live a disciplined life, so he looked for a way to rid himself of his unwanted "gift."

His answer came when priests arrived in his Delta area, wearing their long black robes and carrying big crosses. The Dene greatly feared these men; it was known their medicine was powerful and they could send you to hell. They could also take away all of your powers, as well as gain the Creator's pardon for all the bad things you did in your life.

Blondin went to see a priest and asked for his help to get rid of his medicine powers. The priest didn't know what to do, so he told Blondin to kneel down and name all of his powers.

"When you're done, I'll pray to the good Lord that they be all taken away," the priest said.

Blondin was surprised, never thinking the removal method would be so simple. Then he started to think about how long his confession would take.

"So, you say I can just kneel down in front of you and tell you of my medicine powers and they'll all be gone?" he asked in amazement. "If that's the case I'll have to kneel down in front of you for one or two years in order to make you understand all of these powers.

"My medicine consists of everything you see on this earth and have heard about. I have powers of the universe: stars, sun, moon, and other planets in space. I have powers for all plants, insects, animals, birds, fish, water, and I can look into other medicine people if I have to. And that's only a small part of it. All of these powers have to be described piece by piece to be understood.

"For you to help me . . . it's a lot of work for just one man. I've got no wife. I don't care where I stay. I'll move in with you and go to confession every day. But you'll have to feed me and give me a place to sleep. I won't have time to work because I'll have to kneel down every day and confess."

The priest backed away from Blondin, at a loss for words. How could medicine power be that complicated?

"I can't feed you. I'm poor," the priest finally said. Then he asked Blondin to kneel in front of him and say nothing.

"I will pray over you not to think about your medicine power, and to use only a small part of it to help the poor, sick people. Maybe that's what your powers are for. But don't overdo it."

Blondin bowed his head and knelt down. After a while the priest told him to stand up and then he sent him away. But Blondin continued to have medicine powers and still felt they were too much for him to handle.

He tried to isolate himself from people but they hung around him because they knew he could help them. He left the Delta area while he was still young, travelling up Deh Cho and settling around Le Gohlini (Norman Wells). Blondin tried to stay away from people but his medicine power kept on attracting people. He was bothered all of his life.

BLONDIN PROTECTS HIS PEOPLE

Around 1910 Blondin was living near a group of Hareskin Dene who were fishing on K'ahbamitue (Colville Lake). One day a strong medicine person from the group went duck hunting by himself. As he portaged his canoe, two raiders from a far-away enemy tribe jumped up from their hiding place and tried to grab the medicine man, intending to kill him.

Instantly, the shaman used his medicine powers to become stronger. He easily grabbed the two attackers by their shirts and carried them to the river. When he came out of the water, the two men were drowned. The medicine man called on his bug medicine and immediately insects came to eat their flesh. The shaman scattered the dead men's bones and then went home to tell his people what had happened.

Even though the people knew the medicine man had only acted to protect himself, they became afraid that the dead men's people would seek revenge on them for the killings. They decided to tell Blondin and the Hareskin shaman about their fears. Would they look into the incident and see what they could expect in the future?

Blondin made medicine and discovered that the two men belonged to a group of powerful medicine men who had come from far away to kidnap someone. "They have failed at what they came here to do. They are really angry and they will try to kill someone to make up for it," Blondin told the people. The people were frightened and asked Blondin and his friend to protect them. They agreed.

The group moved to a long point of land and stayed there all summer. The two shamans moved away from the group and gave instructions that no one was supposed to interrupt them. They would go into a trance state in order to use their powers to protect the people.

During the following two months the people went about their lives, occasionally catching glimpses of the shamans walking on top of the water and shouting and talking to someone invisible.

Finally, when the snow came, the two shamans rejoined the main camp. "Those dangerous people have left the country," Blondin told the people. "You can go in the bush now and hunt wherever you want. Don't be afraid."

The people were thankful for what Blondin and the Hareskin shaman had done for them. The two were well supplied with food that winter.

BLONDIN TRAVELS WITH MEDICINE

Some medicine people, like Yamoria, Echsone, and Blondin, could spirit travel. If something important was happening, Yamoria could travel hundreds of kilometres in a matter of minutes. He used his power to instantly go where he wanted.

The storytellers say wolverines can travel magically too. The sly animals can fold the earth in half, like a piece of paper, and take only a few steps to get somewhere far away. That's why, if wolverine wants to steal from you when you hunt or trap, he will stay close to you no matter how far you travel. Wolverine never gets tired because he folds the land and takes one step for your hundred.

Blondin too had this travelling power, and one time he used it in a competition called to catch a moose. As the big animal ran away from a group of hunters, the chief challenged them to use their medicine power to catch it. About thirty people took off after the moose but Blondin took one step and caught up to the moose easily. By the time the first hunter reached him, Blondin had killed and butchered the moose and was already cooking it.

When Blondin got older he stayed around the Le Gohlini (Norman Wells) area, where everyone depended on moose and rabbits for food because there was no fish lake nearby. He had a big family with a lot of grandchildren and, even though he was so old he could barely walk, he always wanted to go hunting with them.

When you hunt with dog teams, the trip back home is quick if your dogs are hungry. Blondin would always leave half an hour ahead of his grandchildren, walking with his cane, saying he would ride in the toboggan when the kids caught up with him. But they could never catch up no matter how fast the dogs ran. The people knew he was using medicine power to get home and they respected him for it.

On another hunting trip, Blondin waited by the campfire while his three grandchildren tracked a moose. The boys returned empty-handed and, sitting by the fire tired and hungry and with a long trip home ahead of them, Blondin felt sorry for his boys.

Later, Blondin's oldest grandson John told what happened: "Grandpa started out walking ahead of us while we stayed by the fire and ate what little we had with us. As soon as we finished we set out to catch up with him. It didn't take long, he was walking so slow. He turned and looked at us and said, 'I will walk ahead of you a little ways. Follow in my footsteps and don't look around anywhere.' So we did that.

"I started to feel sort of dizzy, like I was drunk. I was very tired and we still had about five miles to go, but everything went kind of hazy and then we were at home. My two cousins said the same thing; they got kind of dizzy and then they were home."

The grandchildren were young and they wanted to know how their grandfather made his travelling magic but they never could catch him in the act.

"He is always alone when he makes this medicine," John Blondin explained. "When we go home in the evening, the trip back home along the shore is long, but the dogs run fast. They want to get home and rest, just like us. Even though he doesn't get much of a head start, Grandpa is almost home by the time we pull up. Always it's like that."

AYAH, THE DELINE PROPHET

In Deline (Fort Franklin) in the early 1900s, a man named Louis Ayah predicted the changes that were to come to the Dene if they did not live by their ancestral laws. He began to talk to the people about religion and the sacredness of life, reminding them to be respectful of the land, to love each other, and not to abuse alcohol and hurt others.

His teachings were powerful and he shared them at a time when people needed spiritual help. In 1928 most of the powerful old medicine people died and many Dene began abandoning their traditional way of life because they had to fit into the new world.

By the 1940s, elders didn't know what to do to help the young people who were lost, who didn't really know themselves or their heritage. Many children had been separated from their families and raised in mission schools, where they were treated roughly and told that the old Dene ways of power were of the devil. They were also punished if they spoke their language—they had to speak English or French. Sometimes, when they returned to their families, they were afraid of their mothers and fathers, who still spoke only Slavey or Chipewyan or other Dene languages and who still lived traditionally.

Elders no longer sat with the children each day, telling them stories to teach them to live by Dene laws. The young people were thinking more about earning money and living the white man's way; they did not want to listen to the old people. The family circle was broken.

The prophet Ayah was born in 1858 in the Sahtu area. He came into this world with Raven medicine power and he owned a wishing pipe, which he didn't use until he was nine years old. At that time, he was living in the bush with his mother and her second husband—a gruff man who treated Ayah harshly.

On a particularly cold December morning, Ayah's stepfather chased him out of the tent as usual to start the fire and make breakfast. Ayah put two fish down beside the fire to thaw a bit while he went to relieve himself, but when he came back a neighbor's dog had crept into the tent and stolen the fish. Ayah chased the dog and gave it a good beating, but it was too late. The dog had eaten the fish and now there was nothing for breakfast. Ayah dreaded going back into the tent.

By this time, his stepfather was up and had heard the dog yelping. "Why did you give a licking to that dog so early in the morning?" he demanded. "It's not your dog. It belongs to the family in the next tent. You might have killed it. You're a stubborn kid and I don't like your bad temper. If you want to act so smart, take my muzzle loader and go out in the bush and hunt. You will eat only when you've killed something yourself."

Children didn't talk back to their parents in those days, so Ayah went into the bush with an empty stomach. After he had walked for some time, he sat down to think.

He knew he had been born with medicine but he hadn't ever used it. Now he recalled a vision he had had when he was younger. An old man had appeared to him and given him a pipe, saying, "When you smoke this pipe, anything you wish for will appear to you." Ayah had gotten a pipe some time later, and kept it hidden in his shirt along with some tobacco and a couple of matches.

"Maybe now is a good time to try it," he thought. He loaded his gun and then filled his pipe and smoked with moose breath. After he did this, he thought, "I want a moose to come."

Within moments, a cow and calf were running toward him. He shot the cow and she fell right beside him. He reloaded his gun and shot the calf. Ayah could hardly believe how well his medicine had worked.

He was too small to skin and butcher the animals so he only slit the cow's stomach and took out a kidney. He left the animals in the snow and ran back to his tent.

He had only been gone twenty minutes and his family hadn't even started to cook breakfast yet. When Ayah pulled the kidney from his pack and gave it to his mother, she was surprised.

From that day on his stepfather treated Ayah kindly. He was even a little afraid of his stepson because he knew how powerful his medicine was.

Ayah also had raven medicine which he used to help people. Raven helped him to look into the future, to know where the caribou and moose were so he could hunt them, and to heal the sick. He warned people to take special precautions if he saw trouble coming. Everyone respected Ayah and flocked to him for help.

When Ayah was about twenty-two years old, he had another vision. This time, a man dressed in white appeared to him. "I am being sent to you to give you a message from the high power," he told Ayah. "You are a good person. You are being picked out to preach to people about God's commandments so they will be good. But don't preach now. I will come again and will give you further orders about what you shall preach. Until then, be quiet and don't show off. If you act wisely, I will come again."

After that Ayah waited forty years for the vision to return. During this time he helped people and refused to marry, even though many women longed to be his wife. When he was over sixty, the white-clothed man came again and told him, "I will come to you often and tell you what to preach."

Ayah became a great spiritual leader and people travelled hundreds of kilometres to listen to him. He preached about God and had his own rosary before priests even arrived in the Sahtu area.

"The Creator has special plans for you living on this land," Ayah told the people. "Harvest the land and make a good living off of it. If you live with the land you will always live well."

Ayah also told people of the changes the European newcomers would bring to Denendeh. He spoke of the diamond mines that would be developed in the future and talked of a disaster that would affect everyone—starvation combined with war.

"There will be hard times for everyone," he said. "But if you keep my word and live off the land all of the time you will last longer."

In memory of Ayah, who died in 1940 at the age of eighty-two, the Deline community built a large house for gatherings on the property where the prophet's little cabin once stood. They began to meet there regularly to talk about the things Ayah had told them. Elders urged young people to go to the meetings as often as they could. Soon the house was crowded with young and old people sharing Ayah's teachings with each other.

Slowly, the community began to change. Some people began to slow down on their drinking and others quit altogether.

Deline Dene used Ayah's teachings and their own culture to help people live better lives. Since then, a lot of other communities have taken the same kind of action to stop alcohol and drug abuse and other bad things. Leaders and spiritual people try to bring the people closer together to help each other once again, inspired by Ayah and his teachings.

Chapter Six

SURVIVAL AND

MEDICINE POWER

CHEELY BRINGS THE CARIBOU TO K'AHBAMITUE

There was a man named Cheely, from K'ahbamitue (Colville Lake), who got a lot of help from the caribou because he had been a caribou leader in his former life.

Yes, this is a story about reincarnation; the Dene of long ago believed people were born over and over again in different bodies. They also understood the soul never dies and that the body is just like the clothes the soul wears during different lifetimes. The Dene also believe human beings were once animals and became separated from them a long time ago.

In this story, Cheely was preparing to leave his caribou body and die, but before he left he called his caribou people together.

"I want to make a deal with you," he told them. "Even if I become a human being in my next life, I want us to agree that we will always help each other." All of the caribou agreed to the arrangement.

Soon after he died as a caribou, Cheely entered the body of a pregnant woman to be born again as a human. But he still kept all of his caribou medicine powers. Throughout his human life, when people were starving, all Cheely had to do was talk to the head caribou spirit, even if the herds were hundreds of kilometres away, and they would travel to the people. Once there, they allowed themselves to be killed for food.

When Cheely grew old and was dying, he made a promise to his people. "I want to leave something on this earth for you to remember me by. I feel like I didn't do enough for you during my life. I'm going to talk to my caribou people and make another deal with them. I want to cut out a big portion of the Barren Land herd and establish a new birthing ground for them. This new herd will always come back to have their calves at a certain place close to K'ahbamitue, where I am buried. The caribou will always come to pay their respects at my grave and will have their calves around here, too. For hundred of years they will come back here. I'll show you a sign. When the first snow comes, visit my grave and if two small caribou are running around it, you will know what I have said will come true."

Sure enough, when the snow fell, the people saw two small caribou moving around Cheely's grave. When the ice froze, a herd of caribou migrated to K'ahbamitue. Cheely died more than sixty years ago and the people are still glad to see the caribou return to his grave each spring for their calving.

HARD LIFE IN THE MOUNTAINS

Medicine power was often the only thing that kept the Dene from starving, but sometimes it was also the reason many people died of hunger, as this story will tell.

Long ago in the Shitah (Franklin Mountain) area, there was lots of game, including moose, mountain sheep, woodland caribou, and migrating arctic caribou. Because there was so much food, many different groups of people lived there.

Mountain Dene relied only on game because there were no fish lakes in those mountains. The people had to work hard to make a living, using stone tools, bows and arrows, snares and deadfalls to kill big game. If they couldn't kill moose or caribou, they got by on rabbits, ground squirrels, or birds. People always shared whatever they had, but sometimes groups travelled so far apart they didn't even know a group had starved until a year later.

But one year, a group of Dene could not find even a squirrel to kill. They didn't know it, but a powerful medicine man was punishing them for something he thought they had done, and he imposed cold weather on them to make survival difficult. Even worse, he made medicine so that all animals would depart from the area where they travelled. Slowly, starvation set in. It got so bad, the people began to eat tree bark like porcupines.

Even though they made medicine to find animals, nothing helped. People began to die, but the group kept on travelling, hoping to find other people who might be able to help them. They never did, and one desperate old man killed his wife to eat. Of course, that only made things worse; and finally everyone died from starvation.

An old woman and her young son travelled far behind the group, having decided to strike out on their own to see if they might have better luck. They walked and walked until they were tired. They had only the clothes on their backs and the mother carried a small bag containing her sewing equipment.

They found a place to sleep for the night, and in the morning the mother cried because she had nothing for her son to eat. She took a needle from her bag and pierced a vein on her wrist, mixing a few drops of blood with snow and heated it up for him to drink. After sipping a few drops herself, the mother led her son toward the low country along the river Deh Cho. As they walked, they noticed a thick patch of willow in a valley between the mountains. They decided to search the willow patch, in the hope that it sheltered rabbits.

Sure enough, they saw rabbit tracks amongst the bushes. "Son, let's start a fire and warm up a bit. I have sinew in my bag and we can set snares at the end of this willow patch. Then we can chase the rabbits into the snares." In a little while, they had caught two rabbits. They smiled and laughed at each other for the first time in days. They might survive after all!

Carefully, the mother cleaned the rabbits and advised her son to eat only a little bit or he would get sick after not eating for so long. They each chewed a small piece of meat and drank some of the broth. After cleaning and drying the hare skin, the mother sewed socks from the fur for the boy so he wouldn't freeze his feet. The next day they found another patch of willows and snared two more rabbits. Slowly they got stronger as they travelled and continued to find rabbits.

Finally, they reached the low country as the days got longer and warmer. The mother made a bow and arrow for her son and by this time he was killing an occasional grouse for them to eat. Soon, it was spring and the ducks returned. They snared a few of those to eat, too.

Finally, they came upon a group of people camping near Deh Cho who gave them food and shelter. The mother and son gave them the sad news about how they had decided to separate from their starving people in the mountains. Later, they found out they were the only ones who had survived.

CARIBOU MEDICINE

Long ago, strong medicine people, or individuals who were advised by strong medicine people, were natural leaders who watched over their people.

A good leader of a Dene group was someone to obey and also fear. If you broke Dene law and hit your wife or child, the leader would confront you and you would have no defence. Leaders with medicine powers dealt with life and death constantly, so if you behaved improperly, your life wouldn't mean much; you could be punished or put to death.

A large group of Dene lived on a fishing lake one winter, but it was so cold no one caught anything. The men realized they would have to hunt caribou if they were to survive and so a medicine man was approached to find the herds with his powers.

After making medicine for a long time, the shaman reported there were caribou north of them, on the edge of the tree line.

The leader decided they should try to reach the herd, so the people started to pack their dog sleds. Most families owned only four or five dogs to pull one sled, and so by the time they loaded up their belongings there was no room for passengers. Everyone was expected to keep up, even mothers who had to look after the children. They carried their babies and breastfed them when they were hungry. There was, of course, no milk or canned food. Mothers were always gathering and drying moss; the mossbag diapers had to be changed often because it was cold and the baby could easily catch a chill.

The people were already in a weakened condition, so after

they had travelled for two days in the cold and not gone very far, panic began to set in.

The leader told his people, "Don't hide anything from each other, or me. If you don't have anything to eat, tell me, and possibly I can find you something to eat. At Christmas time we will return and trade our furs. We just have to get through this hard time. We must have a cup of flour here and there. Try to help each other out so no one will starve."

Then he turned to the shaman and said, "We have travelled for two days, but we've seen no sign of the caribou. Two more days of travel could put us in real danger of starving. I want you to make medicine and be sure there are caribou close by."

Once again the shaman made medicine, singing and talking under his breath for a long time. "There are caribou just ahead," he said finally. "In fact, I talked to the caribou leader and there is also a muskox herd nearby. So, don't worry. We will find the caribou." The people thanked him and their spirits were lifted. "We will eat well again, very soon," they thought.

The next day, however, still no caribou were sighted. The people were hungry and depressed. In the morning, the leader got up early and prepared the rations he had gathered. He had about ten pounds of flour in a large pail and he made some soup with it.

"We have to keep going," he shouted to the people. "Every family, bring your cup or a big bowl. Here, I will serve you!" So the people brought their containers to their leader and he gave them a bowl of soup, one lump of sugar and a three inch strip of dry meat. Then he urged them on.

The large group tired easily and it wasn't yet noon when they had to stop to camp again on a long lake. Here, they found old caribou tracks. The people got excited and the leader told the women to set up camp while the men went hunting.

That day the hunters found fresher tracks and followed them. The hunt in the deep snow was difficult, especially because the men were so weak, but they killed ten caribou. The people rejoiced when they saw the fresh meat and they fed their families a bit of it. A day later, they moved close to a large herd and started to eat well again. Even their dogs ate well. They made great bundles of dry meat and pounded meat with bone grease.

When the weather turned warm, they returned to their camp on the fish lake with loads of dry meat on their backs. They had to make double trips to transport it all.

Their strong leader had kept them going when they'd wanted to give up, and though they had doubted their medicine man, he had been right about the location of the caribou all along.

ORPHAN CHILD FINDS HIS MEDICINE PARTNER

Storytellers say animals have medicine powers and they often help human beings with it, acting as their spirit partners.

The Barren Lands Caribou use medicine power to help them migrate every year more than 1,600 kilometres to the south, and then back to the north again for calving. Humans can't understand why they do it; they say caribou have good food to feed on in one spot and they don't have to make the migration.

Dene storytellers say it is medicine law that keeps the caribou travelling to a special birthing ground where wolves and hunters do not bother them. This is a place where medicine power is established for them and it keeps them strong and healthy. That's why they haven't become extinct like so many other animals. To this day here are huge herds of Barren Lands Caribou in Denendeh.

When the caribou migrate north in the summer, sometimes

the land is so dry and rough it hurts their feet. When that happens, storytellers say the caribou can make it rain to soften the ground and make the trip easier. People who have caribou medicine power say that the herd meets with their leader before a long journey, looking into the future with their powers and checking on the attitudes human beings have toward them in the areas they are going to pass through. Sometimes they avoid areas where people who failed to show them proper respect are living.

Years ago a group of Dene was camped near a small fish lake. When the coldest winter in years hit their area, the fish in the lake died until their nets caught only one of two fish a day.

The people waited for the caribou to pass by on their annual migration, but that year they didn't come. Soon the people began to starve, but no one was weaker than one frail ten-year-old boy who became very sick. He was an orphan, but no one had ever told him about his real parents.

One night as he sat by the fire, almost delirious with hunger, his foster father sat down beside him and offered him a mouthful of fish and broth. "Eat this, this is all that we have," he told his adopted son, feeling helpless. The father felt it was time to tell his son a little bit about his past before he died.

"My son, when you were a baby, you survived a war with your medicine power. Your real parents were killed. We took you in and raised you as our own son, expecting you would help us with your powers when you got to be an adult. But things haven't worked out that way. Now it looks as if we will all die."

The boy listened to his father and then curled up to fall back asleep. But as he lay there he thought, "Why didn't they tell me before that I was adopted, and I had medicine power? Maybe I could have done something about this situation." Through the night the boy began to feel his power—caribou medicine. He sent a message to the caribou leader hundreds of miles away, begging the herd to pass near his camp. The caribou agreed to pass by the next day.

As the boy waited, he looked into why the caribou hadn't come that year. He found out that farther north, a powerful shaman who hated the boy's people for unknown reasons, had cursed them. He had placed an invisible barrier around their camp to prevent the herd from passing close to them.

Early the next morning, the boy asked his foster father to tell the people to get their caribou snares and set them among the trees in the valley. The boy went back to sleep until noon, when he got up and walked outside for the first time in many days. The people watched him as he slowly walked, using a stick to lean on, across the lake ice toward a small island. The boy was singing a strange song and a small animal, like a dog, ran circles around the boy's legs.

Suddenly, toward the north came the sound of a loud explosion. As the people watched, they saw a huge herd of caribou appear at the end of the lake, moving toward their snares. The boy had succeeded in knocking down the invisible barrier the evil shaman had erected.

Joyfully, the people removed the caribou from their snares and roasted a little of the meat, eating only a few mouthfuls at a time until their stomachs could adjust to digesting food again.

The little boy, angry at the way the evil shaman had made his people suffer, made medicine with the caribou leader to make sure no one else would be hurt by him. They found the medicine man had powerful medicine over caribou, but together the boy and caribou leader found a way to override him.

"We will kill this man for you. He is not a good human being. He has murdered a lot of people in his time," the caribou leader told the little boy. And sure enough, news came to the boy's camp later that the bad medicine man had been killed in a caribou stampede while hunting.

MOOSE MEDICINE POWER

Though he may look clumsy and dull, the moose is a smart animal. If a moose is attacked by a hunter, he never forgets it. He will find his own way to protect himself for the rest of his life. Moose even use different survival "techniques"; for example some always run downwind and look back on their tracks, others move in a circle around their eating place and bed down where they can smell and hear approaching hunters.

If a shaman has this animal as his or her medicine partner, the moose demands they follow strict rules. Sometimes medicine people overdo things and the mistake costs them their lives, as it did in these stories.

A hunter from a large camp living on Sahtu (Great Bear Lake) was once assaulted by two men from an enemy tribe. While the rest of the raiding party hid, the men attacked the hunter as he packed his canoe on the river bank, but the hunter quickly summoned his medicine power and killed them.

Enraged, the remaining marauders skulked around the hunter's camp, waiting for a chance to avenge their partners' deaths. As a result, the hunter's people were afraid to leave their lodges to go hunting or fishing and they begged their two powerful medicine people, one of whom was the hunter, to protect them.

The shamans went to work making medicine to take away the enemy's weapons and the tools they used to hunt and fish, knowing they could not survive without them and would have to return home.

The hunter announced he was going to take the eyeballs out of the lead bushman's head to teach him a lesson. "He is a strong medicine man, but I have moose-head power over him, so I can override him," he told the other shaman. But his partner was doubtful.

"Are you sure of what you're doing?" his friend asked. "What you want to do is against the system of moose medicine power. I'm afraid if you go ahead, the medicine will backfire on you."

But the hunter went ahead and used what he called the "moose-spirit-eyeball" to impose blindness on the head bushman. Sure enough, the bushmen left the area to return home with their sightless leader, and the hunter's people were thankful.

A year later, however, just as his friend had feared, the hunter himself went blind. Neither his great powers nor the powers of anyone else could restore his sight.

SPIRIT OF FIRE

The Dene created their own culture to survive, just like all people of the earth have had to do. Perhaps the Dene couldn't have managed to live as well as they did in the cold of Denendeh if they did not have medicine power.

Before European settlers came to Denendeh with their inventions that made life so much easier and more pleasant—like kettles and guns and black tea—the Dene didn't know what they were missing. They got along fine, but today we think they were just surviving.

Even with supernatural forces helping them, life was still hard. Take fire, for instance. Shamans with special medicine powers started fires for the people, but once it went out they would have to ask him or her to light another one.

A shaman with medicine for the sun let the sun heat a pile of dried wood until it burst into flames, just as the medicine person with thunder power caused lighting to strike wood and make fire. Another shaman called upon to start fires had power for the sparks that rocks make when they rub together in a landslide.

There is a story of how one shaman taught his people to make fire without having to call him. "I am going to get some special rock so you can start fires yourself," he said, and went into the bush. He brought back special rocks, known as "cleh" to the Dene. He cracked two of these rocks together over a small pile of dry grass and brush and the sparks ignited it.

After that, a few people always carried two of these special rocks with them to start fires. This is the way it was done until the Europeans came to Denendeh and brought matches.

Chapter Seven

MEDICINE AND

TRIBAL CONFLICT

YALEE MAKES WINTER

Long ago in Denendeh, tribes would war against each other for hunting territory or to establish superiority over all others, especially when medicine leaders were involved.

Smaller groups travelled over the land, looking for war or to kidnap members of their enemy's tribe. The stealing of children was considered to be the best revenge because they were, and still are, so loved and coveted in Dene society, and they brought new blood into their captors' tribe.

These small raiding parties were usually led by a powerful shaman. Before a camp of people was attacked, the leader made medicine to see if there were shamans amongst the enemy who could overpower his group. In this story, the leader's investigation was inaccurate and Yalee proved to be a formidable opponent.

Yalee's people were living on the shore of a timberline lake on a caribou migration route. It was summer and the people were busy working and drying food for the winter when they became aware of an enemy watching them. They could hear whistling and their dogs barked steadily, yet no one ever caught sight of the them.

As time went on, the attackers became fearless and crept into the people's tents at night, stealing cups, axes, knives, and muzzle loaders. If they found women alone they would rape them. Soon Yalee's people had nothing to eat because they were afraid to go hunting or fishing.

The people became desperate and visited Yalee's lodge to ask his help. Yalee made medicine to check into the bushmen's medicine powers, reporting that the leader and two other tribesmen had great supernatural abilities and were not afraid of anything.

"They hope to rob us, and will possibly try to kidnap a few of our children," Yalee told his people. "I will look into what I can do to help you when I sleep tonight. In the morning we will gather again and I will tell you everything I have found out."

The next day, Yalee told his people the enemy was not out for blood. "They want to steal a few things from us and take some of our children. They have strong shamans among them. I can't match them, but I'll try to do something they don't have medicine for." The people answered they would go along with anything to get rid of the intruders, because they certainly did not want to lose any of their children.

It was the middle of summer, but Yalee intended to make it winter. "I'm going to make cold weather and we all have to suffer through it, not just our enemies. Right now they are far away from us, but they will be back tonight. Use this time to go home and bring out all of your winter clothing. Mend your coats, leggings and mukluks if they need it and then dress for winter. Collect all the firewood and food that you can and gather in your tents so no one is left alone.

"Don't be scared. In time, the cold weather will force the enemy to go back where they came from," Yalee added.

The next day a north wind started to blow. Two days later, the weather started to get cold and by the third day, the small lakes had begun to freeze. It was so cold the people had to keep their fires going all day. Two weeks later, all the leaves had fallen off the trees and were blown away; the world looked and felt like the middle of winter, even though it was the time for summer.

Finally, the people asked Yalee to see what had happened to their enemies. Yalee made medicine and then told them the enemy had left.

"There's no one around. I am not sure if they made it all the way home. I tracked them back north a long way, so you don't have to worry about them finding you if you travel to hunt caribou. The snow will melt a bit now and then winter will be here again. So do your work and quickly forget about the bad men."

Yalee protected his people to the best of his ability. He knew his enemy was stronger than he, but he still managed to use one of his powers for which they had no defence. Unfortunately, even his own people had to suffer because of the cold weather method he used.

SKULL ISLAND

As I mentioned earlier, long ago the Chipewyan tribe was the biggest and most powerful in Denendeh long ago. There are stories about the Chipewyan travelling and living as far south as the Peace River area and as far north as the Barren Lands. There are Chipewyan people as far east in what is now known as Saskatchewan and scientists recently discovered the remains of a Chipewyan camp between Sahtu (Great Bear Lake) and Aneky Conhon (Coppermine).

This story is about a small war between groups of Chipewyan and Dogrib people who were both living on Tucho (Great Slave Lake). At that time, the Chipewyan occupied the north side while the Dogrib lived and fished on the south side. Tucho is huge, maybe 300 kilometres long, and both groups had picked a certain point of land to mark the boundary between their fishing areas. Both tribes often had spies living with the other group; they could speak both Chipewyan and Dogrib languages and disguised themselves as poor people. In this story, after a large group of Dogrib travelled too far into Chipewyan territory, a Chipewyan spy was sent to live amongst the enemy.

"The Dogrib are living on an island in the lake," the spy reported. "They're not far from the mainland but they think they are safe from attacks. They are well armed and they talk every day about how strong they are and that they hate us," he added. This enraged the chief and so he gathered some of his best men to help him plan an attack on the Dogrib while the spy was sent back to his post.

One night, while the Dogrib camp slept, the spy crept out of his tent and cut holes in every one of his enemy's canoes with his sharp knife. Then he silently moved to the end of the island so he could signal a big group of Chipewyan who were hiding in the bush on the mainland. He set fire to some hide tied to a long pole and waved it back and forth; immediately his people rushed to their canoes to cross over and attack.

Storytellers say everyone in that Dogrib tribe was killed that night. Some tried to escape in their canoes but they drowned when the water came through the holes the spy had cut in them.

For a long time after that attack, the island was littered with the skulls of the Dogrib people and so it was named "Skull Island."

GRIZZLY BEAR SURPRISE

When the world was new, you could never quite be sure who you were talking to and what might happen next. You never knew if the person you were dealing with had a lot or very little medicine power.

Near Tthebachaghe (Fort Smith), a man no one knew very well was fishing on a river bank, minding his own business. A bad medicine man approached him and shouted at him, "You! I don't like you. I will kill you with medicine because you have given me a hard time, speaking against me in public."

The poor man was surprised. "What? Is something the matter with you? What have I ever said about you? Do you mean what you say?"

"Yes, I want to kill you," the bad medicine man repeated.

The poor man said, "All right. We will go around that small point, it's not far away. Follow me."

They walked around the point and there was a huge grizzly bear asleep in a small opening between two rocks. The poor man looked at the medicine man and told him, "All right, if you want to kill people so badly, you can kill this bear first and me later."

While he was talking the bear stood up, roared, dropped to the ground and walked toward the bad medicine man. The shaman was in shock. He turned around and ran away.

People who knew him said he never tried to terrify anyone again.

SPIRITS ON GOAT MOUNTAIN

A group of Mountain Dene was travelling over the mountains, heading toward Yukon Territory to exchange furs for European goods, when they began to hear strange noises. They were near Goat Mountain, a famous Dene "medicine power" landmark that rises higher than all the other peaks around it, when the low voices and high-pitched whistles began.

The people asked four medicine men in their camp to investigate who was following them and what were their motives. After making medicine, the shamans discovered they were being pursued by many men who wanted to kidnap some of their children.

When the Mountain Dene heard this, they panicked. Women no longer ventured out to pick berries or gather firewood and no one set rabbit snares or hunted. Their shamans also found that the stalkers had used red fox medicine to erect a supernatural "fence" that imprisoned the Mountain people's spirits.

Sure enough, the Mountain Dene had noticed a red fox lurking in the bush around their camp. Since the stalkers could do anything they wanted with the people's spirits, the Mountain Dene feared death was not far off. They begged their medicine people to break the "fence," but to do that they needed to find someone with red fox powers. When one of their shamans revealed he had this power, he led the other four in making medicine to break the fence.

When it was done, one of the shamans told the people, "You're okay for the time being. We are lucky to have found a loophole in the stalkers' medicine. They're camped right on the peak of Goat Mountain and they don't have medicine powers for that mountain. We're going to imprison their spirits up there to stop them from bothering us."

The medicine people asked some of the hunters to cut four big spruce poles to erect like a tipi frame. They explained that the point where the poles were tied together would represent the peak of the mountain when they made their medicine to imprison spirits on it.

The hunters cut the poles and returned to camp to erect them, following the shamans' directions closely. One man began to climb to the top of the five-metre high frame, but fell to his death before he could secure the poles. The people became afraid that the medicine-making was backfiring, since it didn't seem reasonable that the man would have died from so short a fall. But the shamans insisted that whatever had been begun must be finished.

After one of the shamans protected himself with medicine and tied the poles together, he joined the others inside the tent to make a ceremony to imprison the enemy. When they were done, they came out to tell the people that the man who had died had definitely been affected by the medicine of the stalkers. "They know what we're doing and they are trying to prevent it," one shaman told them. Then they went back into the medicine-making session.

Finally, all five shamans came out to announce the deed was finished. "The stalkers won't be following us any more," the red fox medicine man told the people. "In fact, they won't be going anywhere. Their spirits are imprisoned right on top of Goat Mountain and they don't have the powers to get down."

The medicine people advised everyone to pack and look for somewhere else to hunt. "Don't be afraid. We are looking after you," they said, but the people were still afraid. It was hard to trust anyone when their lives were at stake. Finally, they wrapped the body of the dead man in hides and placed it high in the trees, and began packing to leave.

After that, they wandered away in peace, and after one night's travel the hunters shot several moose and everyone ate well. While the people were all feeling good again, the medicine people called for a meeting.

"We feel we have to straighten things out with the people whose spirits we imprisoned," the red fox shaman announced. "They gave us a hard time, killing one of our people, but we shouldn't repay a wrong with a wrong. If we leave their spirits on Goat Mountain, they will die. No one can live without a spirit. We want to make a way for their spirits to come down. If they follow us again to harm us, we will deal harshly with them. But, we have to give them a chance."

So, the group made medicine for the stalkers to come down off Goat Mountain. "We'll be on the lookout for them, don't worry," the medicine group advised their people. "We don't think they'll come after us, now that they know how we're able to protect ourselves."

The fight between the Mountain Dene and the stalkers could have caused a lot more deaths had it continued. Even though the Mountain Dene never came face to face with their attackers, they believed what their medicine people told them; the invisible war going on with medicine power was very real to them.

MEDICINE BROTHERS

Told by Jonas Lafferty, Behcho Ko (Fort Rae)

This story happened around 1890 in the K'ahbamitue (Colville Lake) area. There were four brothers of the Hareskin Tribe who were close in age and lived near each other. These brothers were very gifted, possessing great Echo or Giant Monster power.

Echo power overrides almost anything on this earth. It gives the owner incredible strength to destroy obstacles that get in its way. Like a monster would, the owner can practically tear his enemy apart and even eat the pieces.

One of the four brothers was attracted to the wife of Moon, who was a good hunter who owned a small amount of medicine power. Moon was extremely jealous about his new and pretty wife and always set his nets close to the shoreline so he could watch her all the time.

The brother dared to enter Moon's tent one day while he was out on the water in his canoe. Of course, Moon saw him. In a rage, he dropped his fish net and paddled quickly to shore. Throwing aside the tent flap, he saw the brother making love to his wife. He grabbed her and knocked her aside, reaching for the brother.

"You think you're the only man who has echo power. Well, I'll fight you with echo power, too," Moon shouted.

The brother responded by grabbing Moon's shoulder and throwing him out of the tent. Outside, Moon's arms and legs shattered as the brother hammered him against the ground like a rag doll. People who came to see what the fighting was about could do nothing to stop the violent echo power fight.

Finally, an elder ran to get the other three brothers. They came and stopped the fight, but they were too late to save Moon from being disabled. His arms, legs, hips and backbone—all were broken. The elder begged the brothers to make medicine to keep Moon alive. Moon lived, but he was never the same again: one leg was shorter than the other and one shoulder was lower than the other. Moon walked only with great difficulty.

One autumn, another of the brothers got into trouble while hunting on the Barren Lands. He had left his family at the edge of the timberline, and just before nightfall he shot a big caribou bull. He was slowly packing it back to his camp when he accidentally disturbed a sleeping grizzly bear in a willow thicket.

The startled bear swung around and with one swipe of its paw tore the man's scalp. Blood blinded him as he sank beneath the weight of his heavy pack. His head strap, attached to the pack, slipped down and choked him as the bear attacked.

Quickly summoning his echo medicine power, the man snapped the braided rope from his neck as though it were a single strand of string. Grabbing the bear by the chin, he twisted its head off its body, and then threw it away. The carcass lay limp at his feet.

Everything had happened so fast. The man slumped to the ground, chest heaving. Blood poured from his head wound and he could see nothing. After a few moments he realized he was badly hurt and that he would have to move quickly to save himself. He tore his shirt to wipe the blood away and then found his torn scalp lying on the ground. He placed it back on his head and then wrapped rags around it. Using a stick to walk, he limped toward home.

Sometime after midnight, the man arrived home, collapsing in his doorway. His horrified wife wrapped him in blankets and ran to get one of his brothers, who was camped nearby, to make echo medicine over him so he would live.

In time, the man healed but his wounds were still visible.

Across his forehead was a long, black, jagged scar and his face was marked by smaller scars. People say he was a big, kind-hearted man, but his looks made him look mean. If you were winning against him in handgames he would look at you and you'd just about shrivel from fear, remembering he had once killed a grizzly with his bare hands.

MESSAGE FROM THE GRAVE

Told by Jonas Lafferty, Behcho Ko (Fort Rae)

Jealousy is a terrible emotion that makes people do dangerous and crazy things. We human beings are mortal and, unfortunately, we fall prey to our egos sometimes; we like to have all the attention.

Amongst shamans, as you've already read, jealousy caused a lot of death when one tried to prove he was more powerful than another. The Creator gave people gifts of supernatural power for survival, but he also gave them free will to use medicine for evil purposes if they chose.

It was jealousy that caused a shaman to kill the youngest of four Dogrib brothers whom he suspected had slept with the woman he loved. That may have been the end of one story, but when the peace-loving family learned of their youngest brother's death, they vowed to avenge his killer.

Because the three brothers had no powers for talking to spirits, they decided to put their medicine powers together and make their brother return to life for a few minutes so they could ask him how he died. When they did so, their dead brother sat up in the dirt and told them the name of the man who killed him, after accusing him of having sex with his wife. The dead man sighed deeply and said he couldn't talk anymore because he had to return to the spirit world.

The brothers were furious and not about to let the man get away with killing their brother.

"We will find him and make him suffer!" the oldest brother declared. "We have medicine, too, and he shouldn't have dared hurt anyone in our family."

The brothers packed and set out to find the murderer, locating his camp some days later. They set up their own camp a short distance away and then went hunting. They killed a caribou and brought it back to their fire, butchered it, and laid out the body pieces before them.

"Now, whatever we do to this caribou body, the enemy will feel also," the older brother said. Together they made medicine, proceeding with caution because they knew they were dealing with a powerful opponent, and began the torture ritual. Into the fire they placed the caribou head, watching the ears curl back, the skin turn black and the eyeballs burst from the heat.

In a camp some distance away, horrible things began to happen. The murderer went crazy, screeching in pain as his eyes glazed over and turned white, his face blackened and his ears shrunk. Around him, people shouted and ran, not knowing what to do to help him.

The brother threw the caribou's front legs in the fire, followed by the back legs, and the murder's arms and legs curled up, his fingers and toes sticking out in all directions. He lay on his back, in agony and unable to move.

"That's enough. Our enemy has paid dearly," the oldest brother said, putting the fire out. "It would be a good time to visit our dear friend, don't you think?" he added.

The brothers found the murderer's camp and saw he was half dead, but they felt no pity.

The oldest brother spoke once more. "So now you see what can happen when you kill someone. You don't always get away with it. There is sometimes a different ending to the story than what you planned."

The brothers left the murderer to die, confident he had no powers to save himself from their medicine and satisfied he would hurt no one again.

THE GREEDY GIRL

Told by Julia Blondin, Deline (Fort Franklin)

It was late in the fall when a chief—a man with small medicine power—received a visit from a family who lived on a fish lake not far away. Though he didn't have much, the shaman lived according to Dene law, and so his family shared everything they had with their visitors.

It wasn't too long before the chief's supplies began to run out because the daughter of the visiting family was overweight and very greedy. Not only did she eat about three times as much as everyone else, she was also uncommonly ugly.

"I don't like that girl!" the chief's wife complained to her husband, but he only told her to keep quiet.

"Don't say things like that," he said. "It can be very dangerous to talk like that about others when you don't know who they are. That's why we have a law that says we have to take care of others whether they are good or bad."

When the chief stuck up for the girl, his wife secretly hated her even more. She watched in anger one night as her husband told the girl, "If you are still hungry there are more fish here. Cook some more, and eat. We'll visit the net again anyway." Almost before the words were out of his mouth, the girl grabbed two fish and threw them in the fire. She burned them a bit and then stuffed them in her mouth . . . scales, guts, bones, and all. The woman watched in disgust as the girl licked the fish blood off her fingers and then wiped them on her filthy clothes.

"Look at her . . . with those mean-looking eyes and long, messy hair. She eats like a hungry wolf!" the wife exclaimed. "Get her out of my tent! I don't want to see her! She's not like other women. When she packs wood she carries twice as much as any man!"

But the chief kept quiet and just watched the girl. He was pretty sure she had medicine power of some kind.

But then the day came when the greedy girl began asking her mother for fish from the plate belonging to the chief's only son. This meant the girl wanted the boy to be her husband. In those days there was no such thing as courting or kissing and hugging in public. If a young boy and a young girl wanted to marry they would communicate their wishes through one of their mothers and she would negotiate the marriage. Or, if a girl ate food off a boy's plate, this would also signify her intent to marry him.

Just like any mother, the chief's wife wanted the best for her only son . . . but now this beast wanted him for her husband! "It's too much," she thought, and started shouting at her husband to get rid of the girl. But still the chief told her to keep quiet, and to remember the Dene law of being kind to everyone. And the woman, like all Dene women of those long-ago times, obeyed her husband.

She clenched her fists and glared across the tent at her husband when she heard the greedy girl's mother say, "My daughter wants your boy to be her husband now." But the chief only smiled back at her. He strongly suspected the girl owned medicine and he was happy to see her bringing her powers into his family. His son was a good boy, but alas, he had shown no sign of having any powers.

The chief rubbed his chin and thought to himself, "When my wife and I are gone, this girl will look after my son and grand-children." Then he drew himself up importantly and addressed the girl's parents.

"Before this marriage takes place, we will have to bring the elders here to decide if this is the right thing to do."

After the elders had gathered and decided, as much out of respect for the chief as anything, that the marriage should take place, the wife was beside herself. Still, she had to keep quiet while her husband advised their son on how to be a good husband.

"My boy, I want you to be a strong person. Don't listen to anyone else, just be responsible in looking after your wife. Try to help each other live a good and happy life. I promise you that in the future things will change and you will have a good wife and be proud of her. If you have problems, come and talk to me pri-vately. I will always help you. I am your dad."

After the marriage, the young couple stayed in the boy's par-ents' tent while her family returned home. The boy and his par-ents checked their nets every day but the girl still ate so much still they could never catch enough fish to satisfy her. The people gos-siped about her greedy ways and thought their leader should ban-ish her from the camp. They pitied their chief and his son for hav-ing to look after her.

But the chief wanted none of their pity. He liked his new daughter-in-law and protected her. His wife and son, however, did not share his love and they often talked about the girl behind her back. The chief had to keep reminding them of the Dene law of kindness and, through his strong words, he kept his family together.

That winter, a raiding party surrounded the chief's camp, shouting threats of murder and kidnapping. The attackers were so fierce, the chief's people didn't even try to fight for themselves. In terror, they ran into their tents, covered themselves with their blankets, and wailed loudly.

When the chief's wife reached her tent, she was surprised to find her daughter-in-law inside cooking fish.

"You crazy girl! We're being attacked! Don't you know we're all going to die!" she shouted at her. The girl didn't say anything, just kept on eating fish. When the chief came in, an idea struck him as he realized that now might be the time to take advantage of his daughter-in-law's powers.

"If you can help us, now is the time!" he said to her.

She kept on cooking fish and he feared she wasn't going to respond to him either. Finally, she spoke.

"Let me finish eating these fish. Then, I will go out and meet the enemy. You tell the people to stay inside, they cannot watch me," the girl told him.

While the girl ate and put on her mukluks and parka, her father-in-law ran around the camp and yelled at people to stay inside for the next little while, no matter what they heard.

Not long after, a noise like thunder erupted from out on the frozen lake and the people could hear loud crying and wailing. After a long time, the noise stopped and all was quiet again.

The girl entered the chief's tent and she was a terrible sight to see. Her hair was tangled, her clothes were torn and her hands were dripping blood. She was in a trance, breathing hard and shaking. Only when her father-in-law spoke softly to her did she begin to calm down and tell him the story of her medicine.

"I was born with echo, monster, powers. It is very painful because as long as I can remember, I have always been hungry. People feed me two fish and they think it's a lot, but it's hardly anything for me. Now, for the first time in my life I have eaten enough. I feel full. I need a few days to be quiet and become normal again. In time, I will become as normal as everyone else."

The chief was overjoyed to hear his daughter-in-law talk about the powers he had suspected she owned all along. Because he had believed in her and kept her fed, when everyone else wanted to be rid of her, his people were safe.

Out on the lake, the wind blew across bloodied snow. A few of the enemy's spears, knives, and clubs stuck up through the drifts. The girl had eaten everything else.

NATIO, THE ECHO MEDICINE MAN

This story about Natio comes from the Sahtu (Great Bear Lake) area of Denendeh.

Before European contact, the north side of this huge lake drew many Dene to fish along its shoreline and hunt caribou in the nearby timberline and north into the great tundra. Dene from as far away as Deh Cho travelled hundreds of kilometres to hunt caribou on the shores of Sahtu, so important was this animal to them. They used every part of the caribou to make drymeat, clothes, tents, blankets, thread, snowshoe webbing, and even canoes.

It's hard to say what kinds of powers Natio had because there are so many stories about him creating miracles. Once, a medicine man in Natio's camp collapsed. The people ran to get Natio, and when he came he sang loudly and clapped his hands over the man's body. A ball of fire burst out of the sick man's body. Natio said it was sent from the man's far-away enemy who intended to kill him.

"He would be dead if I wasn't here to help him," Natio told the people as they helped the revived man sit up. "Now, I can't send this ball of fire back to the owner because I want to avoid killing anyone. I will send it to the great void, where nothing lives and where no one can ever get it back to cause harm." And so he did.

Another time, dread filled Natio's people as they awaited an attack by a group of strong medicine people who had encircled their camp. Their own medicine people had already tried to get rid of the attackers, but their medicine was too weak to stop the powerful strangers.

In desperation the people approached Natio, who lived away from the camp and kept to himself. They asked him to take pity on them and use his strong echo power. After they begged and shouted at him for a long time, he agreed.

Natio told everyone to stay inside their tents no matter what they heard, then he walked into the inky blackness of the night to face the enemy alone. Not long after, they heard a mighty voice ring out. "My name is Natio," the shaman yelled.

For two hours the people listened to shouting, screaming voices and the sounds of combat. Finally, the noises died down but Natio didn't come home until daylight. The people who saw him return ran to hide from him because he was in a vicious, trancelike mood.

Towards evening he calmed down, but he told no one what had happened. There were no more sounds coming from the bush and no trace of the enemy, except for blood smeared on the grass and rocks. The elders said Natio had eaten the strangers, using his echo power.

After that incident, few dared to bother Natio's people. But some years later his powers were needed again when a quarrel broke out between a hunter who had a large family and a bad medicine man. As the argument grew louder and louder inside the hunter's tent, his wife burst out and ran to find Natio, throwing herself at his feet.

"Natio, please, do something!" she begged. "That monster

arguing with my husband has just told him he won't live long. Natio, I have young children and I love my husband. Please do something before he gets killed!"

Natio agreed to intervene, especially since the evil shaman had killed Natio's friend months before and needed to be dealt with. Into the tent Natio stomped, grabbed the medicine man by the hair and threw him outside onto a woodpile.

"I don't want to see you in this country anymore," Natio roared at him. "Because of you, I have lost a good friend. No one wants you and your evil deeds around here anymore. I am going to go easy on you and spare your life. Just turn around and walk into the bush, now! Keep going. If I find you here again, I'll kill you with my bare hands."

No one saw the bad medicine man again.

Natio lived to be so old he could hardly see or hear. His people took care of him, and always took him along when they went hunting and fishing. One autumn they travelled to a lake that was known to have lots of fat fish, yet people avoided it because it seemed to be cursed. Many had died there, killed by ghosts or strangers lurking in the bush.

When the people checked their nets, they were full of fine-looking fish, but that night as the first snow fell, they heard strange noises around their tents. Though they knew the stories of bad luck that had befallen people at this lake, they had thought they would be safe because Natio was with them. But now, as fear gripped them, they gathered in one tent, afraid for their lives.

Someone explained what was going on to Natio, who sat in a corner; then they listened carefully to what the old man had to say.

"I know I am going to die in this place, so I will help you people once more. Put me in my old caribou-hide toboggan and wrap me up so that only my head sticks out. Take me to that high hill that overlooks the lake, and then push me down the hill. Just let me go."

That night, in the darkness, the people pulled Natio to the top of the hill. From there, they pushed him down, thinking that he would die when he reached the bottom of it and they would not see him alive again. But soon they heard Natio's voice booming far below, and then there were other loud noises. It sounded like many people crying and yelling at each other as Natio used his "giant monster" echo power to destroy the ghosts who had been bothering people.

After a long while, the noise died down and the people heard Natio shouting to his grandson that he was going to die. "Come to me and we shall say our last good-bye. Then you will bury me here and name this hill for me."

Natio was buried along the face of the mountains, east of Rampart Falls near the site of today's Fort Good Hope. His burial site was often named by long-ago storytellers as "Echo Weti— Giant Monster's Sleeping Place." A few elders around Fort Good Hope would still be able to point out the landmark, but it's so far out of the way that most modern Dene don't know where it is.

A SMALL CONFLICT DEVELOPS INTO A LONG WAR

In their continued hunt for food, many Dene tribes travelled endlessly over the Barren Lands following the caribou migration routes. One summer a group of Chipewyan met some Hareskin people and immediately a conflict over medicine power arose.

The powerful Chipewyan people killed about ten Hareskin hunters and then went back home. But they returned the next year to destroy even more. However, this time the Hareskin people were ready for them. They too had powerful medicine people amongst them, who foresaw that a group of thirty Chipewyan warriors had left the main group and was on its way to attack them.

That night, the Hareskin hunters silently entered the smaller Chipewyan camp and killed all but ten warriors, who escaped into the night. Three Hareskin shamans made medicine so that the escaped men would starve before they reached the main camp and reported the massacre.

The shamans sent a fox to frighten off any game that the Chipewyan might hunt. If a warrior aimed at a ptarmigan, the fox scared it away before he could shoot. After five days of this, one warrior died and the other nine found themselves on a point of land surrounded on three sides by water. Lost, and having to back-track for miles to get home, the group knew death was near.

To seal their enemy's fate, the Hareskin hunters had also managed to remove almost all of the Chipewyan warrior's medicine powers.

"This power our enemy has over us is very strong," one of the Chipewyans said. "I will die too, but I might be able to use my wolf medicine to travel home and at least tell our people what happened to us."

The man changed into a wolf and ran away, helpless to do anything but leave his friends to die. He swam across the lake and arrived home many days later. He told his tribe the terrible story and then became weaker and weaker until he died. The Hareskin people were too powerful even for his wolf medicine.

The Chipewyan were furious and vowed to gain revenge on their enemy the following summer. Thus began the long history of wars fought between the Chipewyan and the Hareskin people.

THREE STORIES OF MEDICINE POWER PROTECTION

The first of these next three medicine protection stories came to me on a cold winter night while I was caribou hunting with some friends near Etacho on Great Bear Lake. An old man, Ka Na Een, who had been following our tracks, caught up with us when we stopped to butcher the caribou we'd shot. Later, although we had a good fire, it was too cold to sleep so we sat up all night and listened to the elder's stories. Ka Na Een had travelled all over the North and had even spent time in the south around Behcho Ko. I guess he knew he would probably die soon, so he was comfortable in telling us about his many medicine powers. Towards morning, I asked him if he had ever killed anyone with his powers, and he told me about the time his friend suddenly turned on him and tried to destroy him. Though Ka Na Een has been gone many years, I still recall how happy he was and how lively he was in handgames. He told me, "You never know who you are dealing with. That's why Yamoria gave us the Dene laws to be polite to each other. Always live by them." I have never forgotten his words.

A DEADLY MISTAKE

Told by Ka Na Een, Radeli Ko (Fort Good Hope)

Two friends were living together and getting along well until one became jealous of the other and decided to kill him.

The more powerful shaman pursued his old friend for three days, chasing and scaring him in the spirit world while the poor soul frantically looked for a place to hide. Finally, the lesser shaman escaped to the outermost of three layers of spiritual energy that surround the earth, called Yah. Before he went, in desperation, he grabbed the spirit of his enemy's small daughter to use against his opponent.

When the powerful shaman found out where his enemy was hiding, he flew to the third Yah, ready to attack. Frightened, the old friend threw the little girl's spirit at her father, who promptly killed her, thinking it was his enemy.

Back at home the next morning, the jealous man cried with his wife when they found their little girl dead.

The poor shaman entered their tent. "You should know who killed your daughter last night!" he shouted at them. "Why do you cry and act as if you don't know? Bury your daughter and then pack up and leave this land! I don't want to see you again. If I ever do, I'll kill you before you can turn around!"

The lesser shaman spoke boldly, knowing full well his opponent could easily overpower him. Fortunately, his former friend was overcome with sorrow and his bluff worked! The man and his wife were never seen again in that area.

HIDING IN THE RIVER

One day Begaule, a man with small medicine power, realized he was being attacked by an enemy who wanted him dead. Extremely powerful, the opponent had medicine for many natural elements on earth and in the heavens.

For days the weaker Begaule looked for a way to defend himself, but his attacker had medicine for everything he came up with so he couldn't use it. He was getting weaker and weaker as his enemy wore him down.

Finally, Begaule went to sit by the river to ponder upon what he might do to escape death. As he sat, watching the rushing current, he was reminded of his river water medicine. Did his attacker have river water medicine? No, Begaule divined.

He quickly transformed himself into spirit so he could hide in the bubbles in the rushing water. As a rule, medicine people will not attack an opponent for longer than three days, so after hiding for that length of time, Begaule came out and escaped the wiles of his attacker.

GLUE MEDICINE

A group of people were camped on a lake catching fish and drying them for the winter when they began to feel they were being watched. At night, their dogs barked constantly so they knew a powerful band of stalkers was either trying to kill them or kidnap their children.

They begged their medicine people to help them. They shouted and yelled at them to arouse their emotions so they could connect with their power.

The shamans went away on their own for a while to contact their spirit helpers and determine how they could help in this situation. Shamans don't have free will to do just anything with their power; for matters of life and death they have to get permission from their spirit helpers before they can help.

Finally, one shaman came out of his tent and told the people he had a very dangerous power he had never used before.

"It's like a glue," he explained. "It's usually used to capture animals for food. I can spread it over an area and it catches spirits and doesn't let them go, unless the animal or person has a stronger power, but that's not likely. It's very strong."

"Oh yes, use it! Please use it!" the people begged, jumping up and down.

The shaman told his people to move to the end of a long point of land. He joined them and worked his power from there, spreading glue medicine at the foot of the point so when the stalkers came looking for them, they would be stuck.

After three days, the shaman looked into his glue medicine to see if he had captured anything. Sure enough, two spirits had been caught the first night. They belonged to spies, who died the next day in their camp.

Immediately, the stalkers used medicine to see why their spies had died. They failed to see that the glue medicine held their spirits, because they had no glue medicine themselves. Bewildered and fearing for their own lives now, they packed and left the area.

Chapter Eight

HEALING WITH

MEDICINE POWER

HEALTH AND WELL-BEING

The elders say the Dene of long ago were generally healthy and lived a long time. Diseases like the flu and chicken pox were unheard of. Today's cancer and other killers can be caused by stress, environmental pollution, and chemicals in food that weren't around then. In those days, many people died natural deaths in their old age.

A doctor would say the Dene lived a healthy lifestyle. Outdoors all the time, they breathed fresh air and got lots of exercise: cutting wood, paddling, hunting, walking, running, and packing their belongings. One of the Dene laws says people, especially youngsters and teens, should be active and not sleep too long, especially in the daytime.

The Dene drank meat broth and pure water, and ate caribou muscle either raw or boiled. In the winter they ate fat, but avoided it in the summer because they believed it made them weak. A tonic that strengthened the body and cleaned the stomach was made from boiled rock tripe, a plant that grows and dries to a crust on rocks all over the tundra. Other plants were used to heal specific health problems.

You might ask, "How could the Dene live so long when they lived such a dirty life, with no soap to clean themselves or their clothes?" All I can think of is the land was clean and people didn't pick up the germs that they do now. I guess a little dirt here and there doesn't hurt you after all.

Dene of long ago also had medicine power working for them

and sometimes grandparents used their powers to make a child live long. You see evidence of this all over Denendeh. The eldest children outlive their sisters and brothers because they were given the benefits of medicine power by the old people before modern generations began relying on doctors and hospitals. These older children might also have lived according to Dene law before the new ways set in. Maybe they ate better food or helped old people; there are many legends about children who helped their elders and were given the gift of long life by them.

Long ago people had different attitudes towards aging and perhaps this also led to longer lives. Elders were active; they were respected and held a place of honour in the camp as important leaders and teachers. Today old people are not as valued; many are put into nursing homes to live out their last days. Feeling worthless, they would rather die than live.

Even though there was little disease in those days, people still hurt themselves in accidents and many became ill because bad medicine had been put on them. When these things happened, the Dene turned to their medicine people for help.

SEAGULL MEDICINE

Tacheam was a man who had seagull medicine for healing and he used it well. People saw him heal a few people and so they followed him around. He was sort of a leader.

But how does someone get seagull medicine? Tacheam explained he got his before he was born.

"I travelled in spirit form on earth and in space and that is when I received my powers. At one time I became a giant. I was standing on earth with my head in the heavens. My head went through the three protective layers around the earth. In the middle layer were all the animal and insect spirits we know of on earth. They were all offering me their services to be a part of my medicine powers. They all claimed they were the best.

"It was the seagull that I chose. That bird told me that with his power I would be able to take out infected portions in people's bodies and heal them. The seagull gave me a song to sing when I made medicine, and gave me medicine words to invoke seagull powers when I needed them."

One spring, as a group of Dogrib returned to Tucho (Great Slave Lake) from the Behcho Ko (Fort Rae) Trading Post, they caught and ate some jackfish for the evening's supper. One man fell deathly sick after eating the fish; he had been healthy until then, and the people didn't know how to help him in the bush. The only thing they could do is help him walk and let him sleep in the canoe when they travelled on the river.

The man clung to life until they arrived home and immediately the group leader ran to get Tacheam.

"Our group should have returned happy, but we're sad. This man is going to die," the leader told Tacheam. "We've seen you often fix people in the past; you have to try to do something about this good man!"

Tacheam said he would try to help the sick man. He began singing his song and talking in medicine language to his seagull spirit partner. Suddenly, he stopped and kept quiet for a long time.

"This man was shot with poison through the jackfish he ate there in the bush," Tacheam explained. "This was done by a man who was jealous over a woman. That's why he got so sick."

Tacheam made medicine again, this time explaining in Dogrib how the seagull would help him remove the poison. Kneeling, he sang loudly and pressed on the sick man's stomach. Then, with a shout, he pulled a long serpent from the man's abdomen.

"This belongs to the jealous man. I will send it out into space where he will never find it again. Then I will ask the seagull to heal this wound. He will be fine."

Tacheam was a good man. He had all of the animal powers to choose from, but he took seagull medicine with which he was able to heal so many people.

BEKAH'S SEAGULL MEDICINE

Another man who had seagull medicine was Bekah, a Dogrib man who lived in the late 1800s. Through his story we learn a little more about how this kind of power works.

Bekah explained the seagull has a special kind of "juice" (the scientific term would be enzyme), in its stomach that can kill germs or parasites of any kind.

In a bush camp, a woman who had been sick for a long time lay dying. Various people had made medicine over her, but they didn't have the right kind since she just kept getting worse. The first priests had arrived at Behcho Ko (Fort Rae) by this time. The woman's relatives had placed a holy picture at the head of her bed and prayed with the Bible trying, to cure her.

The woman could no longer sit up and her relatives began to cry and moan, afraid that she would die. During the Bible prayers Bekah sat smoking his old pipe and frowning. People thought he was an odd person and no one talked to him very much because they knew how powerful he was.

Suddenly, an elder noticed Bekah slumped in his chair and almost asleep. "Why don't you pray with us?" the elder said loudly. "You think you are a strong medicine man so you are proud. If you are so strong, help this woman!"

Some medicine people have quick tempers, especially when someone yells at them. Bekah was so angry at the elder's loud accusation that he jumped up, grabbed the holy picture, and threw it into the fire.

"This will not help you! Such praying will not help you! We need action!" Bekah roared. He began to invoke his seagull medicine powers and asked for a knife. The people thought he was going to kill the woman, but he only cut her clothes and exposed her stomach. Singing loudly, he passed his left hand into her body and pulled something out.

The people could see Bekah was holding hundreds of small, wriggling bugs. "This is what she was sick with. I am going to kill them," the shaman said, spitting into his hands. The bugs stopped wriggling and he brushed them into the fire.

"Get me a cup of water," Bekah said and then started to sing again. He spit into the cup and stirred it, handing it to the woman to drink. She drank, and Bekah stopped singing.

"I took out most of the bugs that caused her sickness and the water should take care of any that are left inside. She should be up in a few days," Bekah explained.

As he had predicted, the woman began to eat and sleep better, and the following week she was up walking around.

Bekah also used his medicine to settle disputes. As I've mentioned before, if a strong medicine person was out of control and hurting people, others could do nothing to stop him or her unless they were more powerful. Some bad medicine people were never stopped and killed many people before they themselves finally died.

During Bekah's time, medicine powers were gradually getting

weaker. People believed the priests who said medicine power was bad and began to rely more and more on the white man's technology to survive.

In a bush camp where Bekah was living, the head of a well-to-do family suddenly became ill. Near death, his relatives asked shamans with small powers to help him, but it did no good. Finally they asked Bekah for his help.

Bekah agreed to attempt a healing, and immediately began his medicine invocation. Eventually, he explained someone from far away had sent a ball of fire to kill the man because he disliked him.

"If no one can get this fire out, the man will die," Bekah said. Immediately the people urged him to work to put it out and Bekah continued making medicine. Pretty soon, he passed his hand into the man's body and came out holding what looked like a small, round piece of glass. It was red hot so Bekah blew on it to cool it.

"When I will throw this into the air, it will go to a place where no one can use it again," Bekah said. He threw the glowing ball up, and it disappeared. Then Bekah began singing again.

"That man far away had no business trying to kill this person," Bekah explained when he had finished making medicine. "I could have killed him from here, but instead I stripped him of all his medicine powers. From now on, he won't hurt anyone."

Bekah told the people the sick man would be well soon and then he announced he would pack the next day to go and visit the medicine man who had lost his powers.

"I will confront him and ask him why he murdered people. Then I will tell everyone not to be afraid of him anymore. They can slap his face and he won't be able to do anything about it," Bekah said.

Bekah had not only cured someone again, he had brought justice where it was needed.

MUCHO USES SEAGULL POWER

Back in the early 1900s, as the old world of tradition and medicine faded away, Mucho was one of the shamans who still had strong powers. With his seagull medicine, he healed the sick and could fly above the land to find caribou.

One winter, when a large group of Dene camped for the night during a caribou hunt, a man got a sharp bone lodged in his throat as he ate supper. He sputtered and choked while the people ran to get Mucho. Mucho entered the tent and immediately called upon his seagull power. He circled the fireplace and pretended he was also choking. He coughed and made it look like he was vomiting, then motioned to the choking man to do what he was doing. Halfway around the fire, the man coughed out the bone. His throat was sore, but he was thankful to Mucho for saving his life.

If seagulls swallow something they don't like they can instantly cough it up out of their throats. This is the part of seagull power Mucho used that night.

Another time, Mucho helped a man suffering from a chronic skin disease. He prayed for his seagull medicine to come and then spit saliva in a small container. He mixed it with water and then spread it on the man's skin. The man's skin cleared up. Mucho had actually created seagull saliva, which is very strong and eats the bacteria that cause disease.

During a hard winter, many Dene were dying because they

could find no food. Mucho was called upon to help and, after he made medicine, he explained a bit about his power and told them what to do.

"A seagull never starves; it can always find food. I asked the seagull leaders to direct me to the caribou. They are two day's travel from here, in that direction," he said, pointing to the North. "You were going in the opposite direction."

Two days later they found a large herd and were able to kill as many animals as they needed to feed all their people.

UNKA'S CURSE BACKFIRES

A Dogrib medicine man lived on the north shore of Sahtu (Great Bear Lake). He had a good wife and many children; everyone loved and respected him. He lived a good life until one day he suddenly fell ill.

His people sent a message to two of the most powerful shamans in the area, asking them to come immediately. The medicine men came and discovered someone had shot a ball of bad medicine into the man. "It's right in your body, that's why you're sick," they told him. "If no one takes it out, you will soon die."

An elder shouted at them to take it out, but they hesitated. "If we take it out, what will we do with it?" they asked. The elders said, "Whoever made that bad medicine must be a bad person, otherwise why is he working like that? If you can override this man's enemy, you can take the ball out and shoot it back to him. He'll have to do something with it then."

The shamans invoked their powers to investigate the enemy;

they found who he was, and that he was very powerful. They also came up with a way to take the bad medicine ball out of their patient, so they worked on him right away. They put him in a sitting position and while one sat behind pressing his hands on the man's back, the other sat in front. Working their medicine for a long time, the man in front moved back a bit and then rushed toward the patient, slapping him sharply on his belly and shouting.

"I got it, here it is!" the shaman at the back cried. The people looked at his hand and saw nothing. An elder yelled, "Make it so we can see it, if you can!"

"We'll try," they said, beginning to make medicine again. Soon, the people could see a soft-looking brown ball in the shaman's hand, no bigger than an egg.

The people were astonished to see what bad medicine looked like. Then, the man who had been sick began to loudly sing his medicine song while one of the shamans put the ball of medicine in a birchbark bowl. Carefully, he placed it on the ground in the middle of the crowd. They could hear the ball moving in the bowl and dared not touch it.

The sick man stopped singing and said, "The man who did this to me is called Unka. I never met him. He lives about two hundred miles north of here. Why he did this to me? I don't know."

An elder again suggested they send the ball back to its owner. "He is wicked. Make it land in his body so he won't notice; see what he can do."

The three shamans made medicine and found it was impossible to return the ball through the air.

"Unka has power for the surface of the earth. He would see it in advance and stop it from hurting him," one of the shamans said. "But we can send it underground so it will come out where he is sitting and enter his body. He has no powers for the underground, so he won't see it."

One of the medicine people got up and cleared the spruce bough floor of the tent. He put the ball in the dirt and joined the other two in invoking their powers. The ball began to make noise and then it slowly sank into the ground and disappeared.

"Unka has the medicine ball in his body. If he can't find someone who can get it out of him, he will die," one shaman told the crowd. "We have finished here now. Everyone can go home."

A long time later word came that Unka had died suddenly. His plan to kill the good man had backfired. And now you can see why the Dene believed in medicine power so strongly; sometimes they saw it with their own eyes.

Today, when someone dies or is hurt in Denendeh, no one blames it on bad medicine because few people believe that kind of power, good or bad, still exists. In fact, if someone is dying of cancer, for example, they travel south to find healers. We have so few shamans left that my people seldom go to them for treatment. Medicine power could help us so much today, but people don't live the strict and sacred way of life that supports it. You must avoid things like television, alcohol, gambling, store-bought food, staying up and getting up late, and gossiping if you are going to attract medicine power; few people are willing to do that today.

THE SWAN REVEALS ITSELF

The swan is a beautiful bird to watch as it flies across the sky in the fall, long white neck outstretched, its snow white body promising winter.

Storytellers say swans are as strange as they are beautiful. They live as long as human beings and some can live to be a hundred years old.

There was a man who never talked about his medicine until he got very old. Even though he was quiet about his powers, people respected him for curing one of his relations when he was young. This man owned only swan medicine, nothing else. Some people have powers for almost everything in the universe: clouds, sun, stars, wind, and all kinds of animals, but this shaman was strong even though he owned only a single power. With it, he was able to look into the future. Mothers brought their babies to him to read their child's future. Wherever he went, people followed him to learn his predictions or to be healed by him.

When the swan shaman became very ill, other medicine people tried to help him, but no one had the right powers to do so. The elders could only tell him to search carefully where his sickness was coming from and then he might be able to help himself.

Gathered around his lodge, the people heard him singing and mumbling to himself in medicine power language. Suddenly he stopped and told the people, "I am going to invite a swan here to talk about my sickness and help me find out what my problem is." When an elder asked him if it was possible for him to make the swan visible to ordinary people, the shaman said, "Yes, I can do that. I will bring him here in the form of an old man, then you will be able to see him."

The medicine man went back to his singing but it wasn't long before an old man appeared beside him, a complete stranger. While the people stared, the two men started to talk together in a strange medicine power language.

Finally, the sick medicine man spoke, "We found out what my trouble is. In the next camp there is a strong medicine man who doesn't like me. He wants to get rid of me because I have swan medicine. He thought he had everything regarding swan medicine power, but he lacks a few things that I have so that I can override him. It would be easy for me to destroy him but my partner says I should talk to you about the situation first."

Several elders said they knew the man the sick shaman was talking about and that he was responsible for the deaths of many people. "Everyone is terrified of that man. You should get rid of him if you can," they said.

After he'd talked to his partner for some time, the sick man announced, "We will get rid of this man!" Soon the medicine making was finished and the swan who looked like a man faded away from view.

In the next few days the sick man regained his health. Shortly after, word came that the strong medicine man in the next camp had suddenly died.

BEAR MEDICINE HEALS ALL

Aboriginal people all across North America honour the bear for its powerful medicine. Storytellers say bears have excellent hearing and are capable of reading our minds; they hear what we're saying and know what we're thinking about them, good or bad. As if that's not enough, they can also control people's thoughts.

The bear is generally a good friend and will treat you the same way you treat it. It has powerful medicine to read your thoughts and know your actions, so if you get into trouble with one it's no one's fault but your own.

Science books say that the bear just sleeps during the winter, but storytellers say bears are very aware during their hibernation. Shamans have discovered that since cold winters make bears suffer, these animals use their medicine powers to help them sleep most of the winter. In the high North, where winters are eight months long, the bear fattens itself with lots of food and then makes a hole or den in the ground to sleep inside.

But even while asleep, bears are using medicine power; they know what is happening on the land around them. If a hunter is approaching the bear's den, it will control the person's mind to go another way. Still, Dene hunters have ways to recognize bear dens, usually by the broken branches and claw marks in the bark of near-by trees.

When a hunter sees a clawed tree, he checks to see how old the markings are. If they are fresh, he knows there's a bear in a den nearby and he starts to think of fat, juicy meat. He respects the bear, though, and will not shoot him in his sleep. He grabs a long stick and pushes it in the hole to prod the bear. When he hears the bear start to make noises, he shouts, "Grandfather, wake up!" A long time ago, hunters crawled into the hole and tied a rope around the bear's neck. It seems like a dangerous thing to do, but storytellers say a bear won't bite you when he's in his den.

Of course, today a hunter will wake up the bear and then sight down the pole with his rifle and shoot. Nevertheless, a traditional Dene hunter will still talk to the dead bear while he's butchering it, praying for the bear's spirit, giving thanks, asking for long life, good luck, and good health.

Storytellers say bears wake up once every hibernation. They open their eyes and say to their cubs, "Let's turn around and sleep on the other side now." The bears' turning action causes mild weather to come, right in the middle of the winter, about the first week of February when the people are suffering most from the cold. Then the chinook or "da tu endah" (meaning "annual dew has returned" in Dogrib) comes and the weather gets so mild there's sometimes a bit of rain so that the trees and willows get soft. Many Dene elders thank the bear for the warm weather and everyone enjoys it.

A long time ago when survival was hard in Denendeh, people called on the bear all the time for help. They believed if you just talked to the bear, and treated bears well, they would listen to you. If you really believed in the bear spirit it would listen to you and help.

The bear bladder is good medicine for sickness. As we all know, the Chinese people also have been using it for centuries in their healing. If you have a headache, stomachache, or sore legs or arms, you should kill a bear and cook some meat to eat. Before you put it in your mouth, talk with your heart mind to the bear about the healing you need. If you are the right person, the bear will help you.

I n the Barren Lands years ago, a Dene shot five caribou and as he hurried to butcher them, he cut his hand on a sharp rib bone. His hand bled and he wrapped it, not thinking too much about the cut since his hand didn't really hurt. The next morning his hand had swollen with blood poisoning and he was in great pain. He and his group started the three-day canoe trip home to find someone who could heal his hand, but the next night as they camped in the bush, the swelling had spread up his arm.

The next morning they spied a bear on a hill. In agony, the sick hunter begged his friends to shoot the bear and bring him the bladder. When they did so, he boiled the animal part in his tea kettle to make a bitter, black juice. He rubbed some of the juice on his swollen arm and then wrapped it in a clean cloth.

As he poured some into a cup, he started to pray, "Grandfather, please help me. I am in trouble. I am sick with pain. Grandfather, you helped people in the past and we believe you still do help the people." The hunter drank the bear brew and tried to sleep.

The next morning he told his friends, "I feel good. There's no pain anymore, none at all." He took the bandage off his arm and it was back to normal.

Chapter Nine

LIVING ON THE LAND

WITH ANIMALS

EARTH ELEMENTS AND ANIMALS

Every culture has its own religion, gods and goddesses and spirits. The Europeans brought Christianity to Denendeh, but before that our spirituality was based on the land. The Slavey and Dogrib of old called God "Nehwesie" (Creator of the Earth) because they knew a great being had given them the planet earth and the use of all good things on it to live.

"We should have great respect for the earth and look after it!" the elders would tell the people at drum dances and gatherings. "We get everything we need from the earth! Be happy. Everything you need is provided for you!" they said. Even though people were so poor, the elders told them not to worry. Then they would start shouting and urge everyone to get up and dance.

It's hard not to be happy when you're dancing. The drummers sing special prayer songs, giving thanks for the Creator's blessings, and then even the oldest person dances; they have to get up to pray. When you get lots of people thinking the same good thoughts and dancing together, it's powerful and the people are blessed with what they need.

The Dene world of old was dependent on the land and animals. Of course, the people respected animals because of the Dene stories about four-leggeds and two-leggeds being our ancestors. Even today, many people talk to animals when they need their help, their medicine.

These are stories about how humans and animals helped each other to live on the land.

SUMMER IN A BAG

When the world was new, winters were much colder than they are now. Storytellers say you could hear the sound of trees cracking and splitting in the icy air. One year, in the Deh Cho Valley, the land was just beginning to thaw out after a very hard winter when, all of a sudden, snow began to fall again. The Dene thought it would be cold for a little while and then spring would take over, but that year it stayed cold.

Pretty soon, people started to worry about having only winter. The snow was too deep to walk in the bush and even the caribou and moose had problems getting around. They have to dig for food with their hooves, and they could have been hunted easily, but the elders cautioned against taking advantage of the situation. "We should save them for the future," they said. "We will need them."

The animals began to starve and people put out white moss, willow tops, and hay for them. It seemed no one would make it through the winter, and finally a big meeting was called for strong medicine people and animals to look into the very unusual weather.

"We have found out that a medicine group has stolen our spring and taken it to the south and left us here with double winter," one of the shamans told the people. "We will use our powers to see if there is a way we can get around them and bring it back."

After much medicine-making and thinking, the group decided squirrel and some other helpers should travel south to steal back the spring. Many days passed before the group returned. When they finally appeared off in the distance, the travellers were pulling a huge black bag. They gathered the same medicine group as before in a circle to conduct a ceremony to help springtime return to the land, placing the big bag in the north quarter of their formation.

After much prayer and singing, the squirrel chewed a hole in the bag and out whooshed the warm spring air. The green season had returned.

Everyone thanked the squirrel for stealing back the spring, thankful that the powerful little animal had the right kind of medicine to do a difficult job.

ANIMALS SAVE A BABY

A Mountain Dene family, travelling in a mooseskin canoe down Deh Cho to Tulit'a (Fort Norman) trading post one spring, hit some wild rapids in a deep canyon. Their canoe crashed into the side of the cliff and broke into pieces.

The entire family drowned except a baby, who, when he had grown big enough to talk told how the accident happened.

"I separated from my body when the boat hit the rock. When I saw my body was not hurt, I went back. Two beaver came from somewhere, wedged me between them and took me to a small ledge to rest. They used their powers so I could behave like a beaver in the water. We swam down the river, resting occasionally until we cleared the rapids. When we got to a wide sand bar I started to cry. The female beaver gave me her teat to drink milk and I was quiet."

The she-beaver picked the baby up by his clothes in her strong teeth and took him to a wolf den. The mother wolf gave the baby her milk along with her other pups. A grizzly bear came by and dropped a dried caribou rib by the den. The mother wolf gnawed some meat off it and gave it to the baby and her pups. The human baby stayed for two days with the wolf family, getting special care. Then the wolf carried him to the riverbank; she sensed that some people would come by soon.

Hiding in some willow, keeping an eye on the baby, the wolf waited. Soon she heard voices and then saw a group of Mountain Dene in their mooseskin canoe paddling down the river. The people heard the baby's cries and immediately paddled toward the sound; they found him sitting by himself on the sand bar. They examined him and found he was all right except for being a little hungry and frightened. They wrapped him in a warm Hareskin blanket and built a fire to heat some meat broth to feed him. Then they washed him off and a woman rocked him until he fell asleep.

They wondered who had left him there, but in that medicine period anything was possible. A couple of shamans looked into what had happened and discovered that the baby was a great medicine person.

"He was with the people we are looking for," one of the medicine men told his people. "They all drowned in the river and only this little one survived because the beaver and wolves helped him. He has great power to have survived."

After the Mountain Dene mourned their dead, they had great difficulty deciding who would adopt the medicine baby. In those days, every family wanted to have at least one medicine person among their kin. The baby was finally given to a middle-aged family. He grew to be a famous medicine man who loved and respected animals and taught children to do the same.

BUSH SURVIVAL

In the 1920s, two Dene families went trapping north of Behcho Ko (Fort Rae) in warm November weather. After two nights in the bush they arrived at Tsoti (Lac La Martre) village, deciding the wives and children would stay there with relatives.

The men set off towards Liidli Koe (Fort Simpson), finally camping beside a fish lake where they filled their nets and shot a moose. They were eating well and each day they went their separate ways to check their traplines, catching lots of fur.

Suddenly, tragedy struck. One of the men carelessly left the door of the stove open as he left the tent for the day. When his companion returned that night he found the tent and everything in it had burned. So he made a small fire to keep warm and waited.

When the careless man returned, the two friends took stock. They had no tent, no blankets, and no dry goods. They were in a pitiful condition, yet they agreed they should stay in the area another three weeks because the trapping was so good. Luckily, the fur they'd already caught had been piled on a stage (platform) in a tree and hadn't burned. With Christmas coming, they wanted to trap even more fur to trade.

At least they still had lots of moose meat and they could always catch fish in their nets. One friend had a bit of tea in his packsack and they rationed that to three cups of weak brew a day; they had to give up smoking because their tobacco had burned. They had a not quite full box of matches between them, so they could only light a fire when they were very cold or had to cook.

The men's bush skills helped them to survive. They also knew their dogs were in good shape and could get them home quickly if the need arose. The first thing they did was build a small brush tipi, packing snow around the bottom and up the sides to make it windproof. They piled up lots of brush to make a bed insulated from the cold ground, and lit a small fire for cooking.

The weather turned colder and the two huddled under a small canvas at night. Every day they inspected their nets to make sure they and their dogs were well fed. They visited their traps regularly and these trips took them away from camp for one or two nights at a time.

"That was the most miserable three weeks of my life," one of the elders who had survived the trip told me. "It must have dipped to thirty or forty below (Celsius) and we had only a thin canvas to sleep in. We spent all our time getting wood, not just small pieces but huge tree trunks that would burn longer. To keep warm we had to keep that fire going all night. We couldn't let it go out or we'd waste more matches. We had to sleep right by the fire and we tossed and turned all night because one side of us would be really hot and the other side freezing. By this time it was December and the nights were very long, but we never got a good sleep."

The two friends stuck it out for three weeks, working hard and eating lots of moose meat and drinking fish broth during the day, but dreading the cold, sleepless nights. Finally, they travelled to Tsoti and Behcho Ko with their furs. Their families had a good Christmas that year but the men had paid for it dearly.

With good bush skills and knowledge of the land it is possible to survive anything. Maybe some day we will have to go back to living in the bush with very little equipment. I say the land will take care of you, but you have to have good bush skills and avoid making serious mistakes like one trapper in this story.

THE BEAR CURSE

One day a young hunter was walking through good caribou-hunting grounds north of Tucho (Great Slave Lake) when he spotted a grizzly bear. Since he was in the wide open Barren Lands, he easily followed it.

The bear didn't like the man being around him so he used his medicine powers to lose him. As the bear approached a long lake he scooped up a pawful of sand and threw it across the water. Then he just waded across the deep lake as though it was very shallow, leaving the young man behind.

Storytellers say that from then on Dene who travelled and hunted in the Tucho area had bad luck. They felt pain in their legs and even their dogs started to limp. As soon as they left the area, their legs felt better. Eventually, a group of Dene realized a curse must have been laid on it so they approached a group of powerful medicine people to remove the bad medicine.

"None of us is strong enough to extinguish the medicine put there by a bear who was offended in the area some time ago," one of the shamans said. "But I have investigated this matter and have found sort of a "crack" in it that people can slip through if they want to hunt in there," he explained as best he could.

"If you want to travel and hunt in that area without getting sore legs, tie a strip of bearhide around both of your legs, and tie bearhide on your dogs' legs, too. That will help," he advised.

Dene who followed the shaman's instructions were able to hunt and pass through the Tucho area easily once again.

THE WOLF WOMAN

Storytellers talk about a woman who lived and wandered by herself on the land long ago. She was a strong medicine woman, but her powers prevented her from having a normal life, so she stayed alone.

Although she looked like a human being, this woman was actually more connected to the animal world. So when she saw a wolf walking toward her one day, she decided to trust him and tell him how difficult it was trying to fit into the human world.

The wolf told her to walk in his tracks for a short distance while he walked ahead, and so she did. Then he went on his way.

Later, she came upon a camp and stayed with the people a short while until she felt that they, too, had noticed how unusual she was. Alone again, she realized she was pregnant from the wolf and soon gave birth to two pups. She didn't want the pups so she gave them to the wolf in whose tracks she had walked earlier.

As she again travelled alone, she hung her head and wondered how she could live a normal life when all these strange things were happening to her. A group of young boys saw her in the distance and ran up to her, saying they were going to have sex with her.

"No one is supposed to touch me!" she screamed at the disrespectful boys, but they ignored her cries as one of them grabbed her by the arm and the others wrestled her down. She kicked and struggled against them with all her might.

Suddenly, as she fought them she turned into a huge rock. The boys were gone too and all around the rock were scattered colourful stones. Later, these rocks were picked up by the Dene for making beautiful, useful implements like carved knives and arrowheads.

Storytellers say that the woman, disturbed by the way the wolf and the young boys treated her, could no longer endure her life and so she used her power to give it up. She was a good woman who chose to transform her power into something useful for humans, even though they had made her life miserable by first shunning and then pursuing her.

TAMING A BEAVER

Years ago, if you were a Sahtu (Great Bear Lake) trapper, the warmer days of early spring would find you speeding across the glare ice of the big lake in a sled. You and your family with a load of beaver and muskrat fur would be heading toward Tulit'a (Fort Norman) and you'd all be thinking about the wonderful things you would buy.

The water has drained through the lake ice by April or May, so it's dry and nice to travel across then. We used to make a different kind of sled to use at this time of year, a sled with runners made of thick boards with flat iron nailed to the bottom so it will slide easily. You can carry a big load on such a sled and move very fast. Put moccasins on your dogs' paws to protect them from the ice and you're ready to go!

One year at this time, a group of travellers found a beaver stranded far out on the thick lake ice. Why and how he came to be there they did not know, but the poor animal was in pitiful condition. He was starved thin, blood seeped from cuts in his feet from the sharp ice, and the fur on his belly was worn off.

The people took pity on the beaver. An elder put the beaver on his sled and said "We will take him to the shore." Once there, the people made a fire and had lunch. The children petted the beaver's head and one child fed him bannock with lard. Her mother cooked flour and rolled-oat soup and, though he was frightened, the beaver was so hungry he ate some of the food.

After lunch, the people packed and placed the beaver on the sled again. After many hour's travel, they reached an area of the shoreline where a river drained into the lake. In the open water, ducks swam and fish jumped. The people decided to camp there for two days to make some dryfish to feed the dogs well and let them rest.

The children made a little hut of sticks on the riverbank for the beaver and a woman cleaned the poor animal's paws, belly and tail scraped raw by the rough ice, and rubbed some fat on its sores.

When the kids petted the beaver, possibly because he was in so much pain, he just stayed quiet and let them fondle him. The children grew attached to him after feeding and nursing his wounds for two days, but then the group was ready to leave. So they packed the sleigh and hitched up the dog team. When the two littlest children cried to take the beaver with them, their grandfather said, "No. He belongs in his own world. If we bring him up in our world, he might die."

The children stood on the edge of the open water and said good bye to the beaver. He lifted his head and shook his tail and then he swam away.

POWER FOR DANCE

Told by Alphonse Lemoule, Behcho Ko (Fort Rae)

When the world was new some people received their medicine powers in strange ways and the powers they received were sometimes useful, sometimes not. There were people who lived their lives never using their medicine powers at all, possibly because they feared them and wanted to play it safe.

Sometimes, when a person received power, they were even told exactly when it would prove to be useful. Years later, when the power might have been forgotten, events in that person's life would occur as predicted, and the person would remember to use it.

One spring, a Dogrib teenager named Bettodea was playing by himself in the bush. A butterfly flitted by and so he chased it until he had been running for hours and lost all track of time. When he finally stopped, he looked around and realized he was hopelessly lost. Too tired to do anything about it then, he lay down on the ground and fell asleep.

Bettodea dreamed that animals came around him and they were like people. They urged him to dance with them and so he did. They had their own drum songs and the boy sang and danced with them all night. In the end, he was given medicine power by the animals for the dance.

When he woke up, it was morning with the sun high in the sky. His parents and friends were looking for him. Bettodea sat up, wondered where he was, and then heard someone calling his name. He shouted back and then the searchers found him and told him how much trouble he had caused.

"How did you get lost?" they asked. "Didn't you know we would worry about you? Are you crazy?"

Bettodea explained, "I got lost and was tired so I fell asleep under a tree."

Bettodea said nothing about his vision, but as he grew older he used to like teaching dances to groups of boys his own age. He would sing drum songs, which he remembered from his vision, and get them to join in.

When the elders saw this they started to talk amongst themselves. "That must be a medicine child to create his own songs like that," they said. "Look at him making the other children dance too."

But they also advised him, "Don't sing and dance like that anymore. Using your power like that might affect you badly while you're young." The elders were worried that young Bettodea might get so strong in his medicine that it would affect his health and mental well-being.

Years later, when Bettodea became a man in the early 1900s, he helped strengthen the tea dance culture. At this time, the dance was so popular it sometimes lasted two or three days. When the people became exhausted and were ready to quit, he would jump up and start to sing his own song. Then everyone would follow him, forgetting their fatigue and having a great time.

In his old age, Bettodea explained his "butterfly" vision to his people. "The animals transferred some of their medicine power to me in my dream. I really didn't know what it was at the time. I was too young and I got a little frightened of this power. I didn't experiment with it. Maybe if I would have, I would have been able to find more good uses for it.

"Animals all have their own song to dance to. If I really cared and was interested I could have sung a lot of animal songs and maybe taught them to the people for ceremonies. But I wasn't curious enough about it. Many times I needed to kill game for food. I wished then I had medicine power for that, then I wouldn't have had such a hard time hunting."

It's too bad this man isn't around today because nobody seems to want to dance anymore. The tea dance tradition that once brought people together in one mind and spirit is weak, and some communities have lost it completely.

CARIBOU HELP

One May, when the snow was melting and the caribou herds were migrating north, a young man went hunting with his gun. Looking toward the south end of a long lake he'd come to, he saw a large herd of caribou moving toward him.

Thinking himself very lucky, he hid behind some willow and waited for the long line to pass by him and then he would shoot one or two. The caribou were very orderly, never veering out of line and always stepping in each other's tracks. They travel hundreds of kilometres that way, the elders say, and they can travel so far because often they sleep while they walk.

The young man was very excited as he waited, his hand on the gun trigger. He saw that the caribou leader was far out in front of the other animals so he waited for the rest of the herd. But then the leader turned to look straight at the hunter. The man froze, not wanting to kill the lead buck.

The long line of caribou stopped while their leader walked over to the hunter, who was more than a little frightened by now. Suddenly, the man noticed the caribou was no ordinary animal. He was smoking a pipe! And then the caribou began to speak.

"What are you doing here?" the caribou asked.

Surprised, the young man stuttered, "I-I-I was just waiting here to kill some of your caribou for food."

"Oh?" the caribou said. "Well, we are just travelling north to a special place where our babies will be born. I came over to you to help you. Here, take my pipe and keep it all of your life. If you are hungry and can't get caribou, fill your pipe and think hard that you want to see me. I will come, but not every time. I will control the meetings we have, if necessary.

"And, if one of your friends is sick, fill your pipe and blow the smoke over the sick person and say, 'This is the caribou breath which helps the sick to get well. Caribou, please help this sick person get well.'"

The caribou turned back to take his place at the head of the herd again, saying, "Yes, fill your pipe and think of me. I will appear for only you to see and you can tell your problems to me. I will help. And . . . you can kill two of these caribou, the last two in line."

That hunter became a special medicine man. He respected the caribou and smoked his caribou pipe only when he really needed help. When people were starving, he would call on his caribou medicine partner. Then the leader would appear to him and tell him where the herds were, or bring them near the starving people so they could hunt them. If healing was needed, the leader would come to breathe on the sick, and even the most deathly illness would be cured.

Chapter Ten

HELPING EACH

OTHER

ENEMIES BECOME FRIENDS

The Dogrib and Inuit are completely different races of people, and in the past they were deadly enemies and often fought each other. But this is a story of how they helped one another.

In 1925, most Dogrib people trapped fur and hunted to survive, as they had done for a long time. They differed from their northern neighbours, the Inuit, in language and in the way they prepared their food and travelled. While the Dogrib used fire to roast or boil their meat, the Inuit ate their meat and fish uncooked because it was so hard to find firewood in the Barren Lands and Arctic Islands where they live.

A group of four people from a Dogrib settlement close to the Barren Lands was travelling in this treeless place to hunt caribou and muskox and trap for fox, wolverine, and wolf. It was winter, just after Christmas, and the weather was very cold and windy. The men carried some firewood, but they had to ration it carefully so it would last during their trip.

When they started they shot ten caribou and thought they were doing well. But the herd travelled a great deal and they failed to kill any more. They trapped as best they could but they ran out of food fast because their sled dogs ate so much.

They made two long trips to the treeline to get wood, but soon they ran out of that too and they and their dogs were getting weak from starvation.

The group became desperate. Joe, the leader, told his men, "It's too far to go back home, the dogs would never make it. It's just too cold and they're weak. I know where some Inuit used to stay. It's about one day's travel from here and I think maybe we should try to find them. If we can't find them, it's just too bad. But if we find them, they will help us. I know some of them."

The other men agreed to his plan and the next day they walked until evening before they found a sled track. They followed it and found an old man fixing his traps. Using sign language and finger pointing, the Dogrib managed to tell the old man what they were doing in his country.

"How far is your camp?" Joe asked him, and the old man pointed to a shiny watch on his wrist and made a sign that looked like "one hour."

"We're starving. Our dogs are starving. Do you have any meat?" Joe asked.

"Lots of meat," the old man answered.

Very quickly, the old man led them to his Inuit people, who lived in snow houses. Joe knew some of the people but he still had to use sign language to talk to them. Pretty soon the two groups became friendly and a big trading session began. The Inuit had been camped in this spot since fall and they had a lot of caribou hides and caribou mattresses. The Dogrib traded their fancy, decorated mitts, moccasins, mukluks, and jackets for warm Inuit clothes and mattresses.

The Inuit fed their guests and their guests' dogs very well. They had a small gas stove and they made tea and boiled meat for them. They had lots of fat meat stored in snow houses, so when the Dogrib were ready to leave they gave them as much meat as they wanted. The men made it back home, feeling healthy and strong.

Even though Inuit and Dogrib ancestors had fought wars and killed and kidnapped each other, these two groups overcame their fear of each other in a matter of survival.

SHARING WAYS

In 1915 life was very hard for the Dene. They were still adjusting to living life partly according to the old Dene laws while adopting new ways introduced to them by European traders and missionaries. Government was starting to develop the land's natural resources of oil, gold, silver, uranium, and wild food, but there still weren't any medical or social services for aboriginal people. The Dene had no white education and few skills to be qualfied for government employment, so they lived on the land with very little.

Two groups of Dogrib lived between Itseretue (Hottah Lake) and Behcho Ko (Rae), about 240 kilometres apart, close to the treeline. The group living farthest north, on a fish lake, was large—about ten families. They were waiting for the caribou to migrate past them at the time when the lake began to freeze, but the herds never came.

Before Christmas five members of this group left for Behcho Ko to trade furs for a few supplies for the winter: tea, tobacco, matches, ammunition, rolled oats, flour, and sugar. They returned after Christmas and by then conditions in camp were bad. The lake wasn't producing many fish anymore and everyone was weak, including the dogs.

They decided to travel away from the tundra toward the trees in the hope that the caribou would be there. The weather was cold and the travel went very slowly. Everyone was walking, even the small children, because the dogs were too weak to pull heavily loaded toboggans. Each night the people had less and less to eat.

There was no food to revive even the children, and so the

group trudged wearily on, desperately hoping to see caribou tracks. Finally, they stopped on the shore of a big lake and made a huge fire to warm their children.

Luckily, their smoke was noticed by a trapper from the Dogrib group living 240 kilometres farther south, who just happened to be trapping on the same lake. He came to see them.

"In my area, south of here, there are lots of animals and fish," the trapper told the starving group's leader. "I am sorry I have only one night's food left, but I will give it to you. It should take me three nights to get home but I will meet you on my way back with more help."

The trapper travelled night and day. When he got home he organized ten dog teams to meet the struggling group with clothes and blankets, fish, caribou meat, and pounded meat with bone grease. It was the best food he could give them.

A week later they brought the poor people into their camp and looked after them, restoring their health and caring for their dogs over the winter. By springtime, the northern group was ready for the spring hunt and, later, they travelled with their beaver and muskrat furs to Behcho Ko.

Back in those days, everyone benefited from Dene law. There was no room to think, "I'll look after myself and my family and everybody else can suffer." Today it's hard to find people who would work for ten days for nothing just to help someone else.

BARREN LANDS RESCUE

When the first Europeans came to Denendeh with amazing new implements like guns, matches, steel knives, and axes—not to mention wonderful food like sugar and black tea—my ancestors valued them. They travelled long distances to trade their fur to buy things that were priced very high.

People sometimes put themselves in danger when they travelled north into the Barren Lands to trap for white fox and hunt muskox whose hides the traders valued. It's difficult to kill caribou for food on open tundra in sixty below weather and there aren't too many fish in the lakes. Depending on the weather and food supply, people easily perished if they weren't properly prepared.

When the caribou were plentiful in the Barren Lands, trappers brought their families with them. Imagine how hard it must have been on the families! Mothers had to bring moss from the bush country to put in their babies' diapers and if their supply ran out, someone would have to travel back to the trees for more. At the treeline, men would have to load as much wood as they could on their toboggans and then ration it to last throughout the trip.

Often fires were lit only for making tea or boiling meat. If the people were caught in a storm with no wood, they had to huddle in their caribou hide blankets for days in unheated tents, waiting out the bad weather. Then the men would have to travel one or two nights back to the trees to bring back wood for fires.

In the 1930s people started to get liquid gas cook stoves. They were heavy, but simpler to use because no firewood was needed. Before that, trappers had to carry a lot of drymeat and pounded meat with bone grease and fat, foods they could eat without cooking.

Several Dogrib families set their main camp on the tree line one winter while five of their hunters went into the Barren Lands to hunt and trap. They were excellent trackers and it wasn't long before they shot twenty caribou, enough to keep their families well fed until their next return.

The men caught enough white fox, which are easy to bait and trap, to make the trip to Behcho Ko (Fort Rae) before Christmas for trading worthwhile. They got a good price for fox and the traders urged them to bring in more muskox hides, so the men returned to the Barren Lands to trap some more. Now it was midwinter and very cold, but the men again found a small herd of caribou and took fifteen animals back to their families.

The men's luck was so good, they decided to move their families into the Barren Lands, closer to the animals. In a terrible storm they arrived at the spot where the men had cached some meat, and set up camp. Right away they had to ration their wood and pretty soon they were burning caribou bones with grease to keep warm. The men could find no more caribou, and quickly the situation turned grim for the Dogrib.

The men killed four muskox but there were so many families the meat didn't go far. As the food ran out, the dogs went hungry and began to starve as the people saved it for themselves. The men continued to hunt but found nothing, so the leader decided they should all return to the bush.

The pitiful group started out for the tree line. It took them two days to walk to the shore of a big lake. Everyone was rationed to a small piece of drymeat and told to suck on it for as long as possible, swallowing only the juice. The people lit a big fire when they had gathered enough wood and they were thankful for the warmth after days of having no heat.

One strong hunter was sent to get help and after three days and nights the waiting people saw a small spot moving towards them far out on the lake ice. It was a different man, sent by the hunter who had gone to find help, and he carried a packsack full of drymeat and pounded meat with grease.

"Three dog-teams are behind me with more food," the stranger told the families, who were overjoyed to see him. Sure enough, more men and dogs arrived that night and so the people were saved.

Chapter Eleven

MEMORIES OF

A PAST TIME

Medicine power was a wondrous thing. When put to good use, it saved lives and uplifted people's spirits. It gave them something to believe in through a hard winter or after a war. But what was day-to-day life in Denendeh like when medicine power was dying out? How did my people adapt to the changes introduced by the European traders and the Christian missionaries? Here are the stories of elders who recall what life was like in the early 1900s, when most people didn't have medicine power to help them.

CAROLINE, A BARREN LANDS WOMAN

Caroline, born in 1900, was ninety-three years old when I interviewed her in Tsoti (Lac La Martre) about her difficult life on the tree line of the Barren Lands. She remembers the harsh winter winds, with no trees for protection, and how everyone depended on the caribou for food because there were no good fish lakes on the tundra.

As a girl, I was married to a trapper by a travelling priest at Snare Lake. I raised many children on my own, I was alone because my husband was often away trapping or trading his fur. I visited Behcho Ko (Fort Rae) only about three times with him in my life—at Christmas and during Easter holidays.

Staying at home all the time was hard. Sometimes we had to travel in the cold and wind with just five dogs to pull the sleigh. I never rode; I remember walking all the time.

We used to stay at a fish lake far south from the Barren Lands. In the fall there was enough fish to keep us going for awhile, but when January and February came the fish disappeared—there were hardly any to catch. Sometimes the caribou would come to winter near us and then we lived fairly well.

In the spring, my husband would go farther inland among the trees to trap martin, mink, and fox, and life was much easier there. In August we would follow a large group of people into the Barren Lands to kill as many caribou as we could to make drymeat, bone grease, tanned hides, and babiche to string snowshoes.

In the fall, all of the men would travel to Behcho Ko, about one hundred miles south. If they really hurried, it would take about ten days to travel there and back for rifle shells, tea, tobacco, and matches. That's about all we could afford.

So that's how our life went, in a circle of work every year. After the men got back from Behcho Ko they would go into the Barren Lands again to look for caribou. If they were lucky they would shoot a few right away and they would be okay. The problem was it was winter by then and it was so hard to keep warm without lots of wood to make a good fire.

Once, we got to the tree line in the fall with four other families. The men went on a short hunting trip right away and came back with lots of meat, but they said there weren't many more caribou where they had been. They were in a hurry to hunt and trap some more, so the next day they left again.

The four other women and I took care of our families with the meat they brought back. Three days later the men returned saying they couldn't find any caribou. They wanted to take all of us up to the Barren Lands so they could hunt and trap without travelling back so far to bring us meat.

It took us two days to walk to where the men had cached some meat. It became very cold and I had five small children to look after. I wrapped them up in caribou blankets and piled them on the toboggan. When we got to our campsite, the men still hadn't found any caribou, although they had trapped a few white fox.

It's very hard to camp in the Barren Lands in the winter. You can't work in the tent and enjoy the heat of a nice fire because there's no wood. I dressed the bigger kids warmly and they played outside for a little while in the daytime. We had only one small fire each day to boil meat so we could eat.

Finally, three men went back to the timberline to bring wood while the other two went hunting for caribou. We five women with our children moved into two tents to save wood. I was the one with lots of kids; the other mothers had only one or two babies each. Most of the time we didn't move very much, we slept in our caribou blankets to keep warm. The two men who came back from hunting didn't kill any animals but they said in one area they saw a lot of tracks so they decided we should all go there.

When we got to the new place, the men went hunting. Then the wind started to blow and you couldn't see a thing for snow. Our meat was running out, we had no more wood and the weather got worse; we had a blizzard for three days and nights. Not one of our husbands got back so we just stayed in the blankets and sucked on drymeat and fat. The kids were pitiful but that's the way things were and we couldn't help it, since we didn't know of a better way to live.

After the storm, all the men got back. They had shot five caribou before the storm and then made a snow house to stay in until the weather got better and they could travel again. We all survived and ended up staying there a long time. The men brought us caribou meat and they trapped a few white fox.

Later, when the days got longer we all went back to the bush and then to Behcho Ko for Easter. That was a horrible winter. The following year we would start all over again. All my years, I went through a life like this. I never complained.

WORKING TO LIVE

This story is told by ninety-two-year-old Pierre Wedzin of Behcho Ko (Fort Rae). He was raised in the traditional way and remembered a great deal about his childhood.

My dad was a Mountain Dene and there were two of us boys in the family. I remember we lived on a fish lake. My dad wanted to make a birchbark canoe so we all went looking for good birchbark. You need bark from a very big birch with no knots in it and we were in poor birch country. My dad said we would have to move camp looking for better trees. So, we had two dogs to help carry our stuff and mom and dad took turns carrying my baby brother. I was big enough to run along with them.

All that day we travelled and found good birchbark, then we went back home. My dad packed a big load of birchbark with a head strap and the dogs packed some too. At home, he put the birchbark in water with weights on it to make it lie flat. He worked hard for a few days to build the canoe. He carved wood ribs to make a framework and then punched holes in the birchbark and sewed it together on the frame with spruce roots. Finally, he sealed all of the seams with spruce pitch.

I remember all Dene families worked hard to make canoes. We really needed them for moving from place to place. Some big families had two canoes—one big one to carry all their kids and a smaller one to use every day for fishing and hunting. It had to be light so you could carry it through the bush from one lake or stream to the other when you hunted moose or ducks.

At the start of 1900 there were people scattered everywhere

in the bush. Behcho Ko was our home community but hardly anyone ever stayed there. You never heard of people working for wages at that time, everyone hunted and fished for themselves to live. The fur trader and first missionaries each had a family staying with them to provide them with wild meat and fish, but everyone else was in the bush.

West of Behcho Ko towards Deh Cho is bush country with lots of good fish lakes; north toward Sahtu (Great Bear Lake) is more good hunting country and the tundra, where the caribou are. Dene camped all over in this area and some never saw white people for a long time, sometimes for years at a time.

I watched people make fishnets from willow bark. You have to work hard to make a fishnet that way. A good provider might have a net thirty feet wide and one hundred, maybe two hundred, yards long with no holes. You can catch a lot of fish then. A poor, lazy person might have a net ten feet long, and torn full of holes. They lived by begging off the good workers. There were a lot of beggars in those days who depended on medicine people and good workers to live.

Everyday, men checked their nets. Sometimes they travelled two nights after moose, or they were out checking their snares for rabbits or shooting ducks, grouse, ptarmigan, beaver and muskrat. Beaver and muskrat were good in the fall for making warm clothes.

Men often travelled fifty to one hundred miles away from home, and were away for three weeks, to kill caribou for meat and hides to bring back to their families.

The women worked just as hard as the men. They visited fishnets and rabbit snares every day when the men were gone. They gathered fire wood, kept fires going, tanned hides to make all the family clothing, and looked after the babies. They packed babies wherever they went, and had to gather lots of moss for their diapers.

To care for their babies, mothers carve and sew a soft birch-bark pouch that fit between the baby's legs and they'd fill it with dry moss; they had to change it whenever it was wet. Women with several babies had to gather a great deal of moss in the fall to use through the winter. They made a special net bag for it out of braided caribou hide string and hung it over the fire to dry before using it. In the Barren Lands, fathers sometimes spent all day going far into the tree line searching for moss. It's bulky and a great deal must be carried back home, but it's all they had.

The other kind of diaper people made long ago was from caribou calfhide, sewn to make a pouch and stuffed with this same special moss. It makes a good diaper because, with this moss, the baby's skin never gets a rash of any kind.

With all of the cooking, drymeat-making, hide-tanning, clothes-sewing, looking after the children, and work with fires, women only rested when they went to sleep at night.

Almost every day there was a gathering so young people could listen to the storytellers, and learn how to become good people. It was our culture to do this. When the speaker talked, no one would interfere or make a noise. They would support the elder. This is how our children were educated.

We also governed ourselves the best way we could. The leader of any group was usually a strong medicine man with powers that could be dangerous, someone whom the people respected and feared. So they listened to him and behaved.

In large camps, there were sometimes individuals who had medicine powers to settle disputes of any kinds between individuals or large groups. This person kept the peace and was very important.

ONE HUNDRED YEARS IN DENENDEH

Helen Rebesca was one hundred years old when she talked to me in Tsoti (Lac La Martre) about her life on the land. Her father was a hardworking, adventurous man who felt strongly about the new Christian religion that arrived in Denendeh in the late 1800s.

I was born out on the land somewhere, I don't know where. My dad was a Dogrib who travelled in the Liidli Koe (Fort Simpson) area where there was a big trading post. The Mountain Dene from up toward the Nahanni River would come down to Liidli Koe to trade furs and my father married a girl from there.

It was unusual for a Dene to travel too far from his birthplace, but my father did. He was an unusual man.

Around 1890 he spent time travelling around the Deh Cho valley, in Tthedzeh Koe (Fort Wrigley) and later Tulit'a (Fort Norman). My dad had a big family and three of his children lived long lives, but I am the only one still living to this date.

After living around Tulit'a, my dad joined the Great Bear Lake people and we travelled with this group called the Caribou Point Dene. I was in my teens when we lived with them at the very end of the lake toward Coppermine. There was a small trading post where we lived and many different people travelled through our area: white people, Behcho Ko (Fort Rae) Dogrib, Barren Lands Dene, and even some Inuit. Some people came over and joined up with us so Caribou Point Dene became a mixture of Slavey and Dogrib with a language that took from both, too. We were isolated but we lived happily according to our culture and laws.

I heard an elder talking about a priest who spoke about God, the Creator. He talked about what the priest preached . . . that you have to be baptized in order to go to heaven. So many Dene wanted to be baptized.

In time, our trading post got bigger and we heard a priest was coming from the coast. My dad was glad, he said, "We will all be baptized!" But then the Inuit killed two priests and everyone was talking about it. Then a year passed and still no priest came to see us so my father decided to take us all to Behcho Ko to be baptized so we would all go to heaven.

We were a big family by then and Behcho Ko was six hundred miles away, but my father was a strong-minded man. We had two birch toboggans, one pulled by three dogs and the other by four. It was winter when we loaded all of the small children in the toboggans and started to travel. We made lots of stops; my dad trapped along the way and set fishnets in good fish lakes. He hunted and we were always making drymeat.

After many weeks, we met other Dogrib travellers and they helped us get to their camp. We joined up with these people. They were strangers to us but they shared everything they had. Our family talked Slavey and now we had to talk Dogrib, but it was okay—it didn't take long for all of us to understand it.

With the help of these people, we reached Behcho Ko by springtime. We children were afraid when we went to see the priest. My father and mother had been married by a priest in Liidli Koe, but we had never seen one before. My dad was really happy when he saw us being baptized. There were eight of us children. I was in my teens and I had two older sisters—they were already adults. The rest were all small kids.

My dad decided Behcho Ko would be our new home. We made our living the same way as everyone else. Some years we would go east of Behcho Ko to hunt and trap in the bush. My dad would make birchbark canoes every summer, one big one for the family and one small one to pack around in the bush. The whole family would help build them.

Later, we left Behcho Ko to travel with people who went deep into the Barren Lands every summer and winter looking for caribou. That sure was a hard life those people lived. They went out in the late summer to collect good caribou hide for winter clothes. In the summer after the calves are born the hides are good—new hair and no warble-fly holes in the female skins. In May or June, caribou bulls develop pouches of warbles between their skin and body, especially on their backs. When each bug grows bigger it chews its way out of the caribou skin and leaves a hole in the hide. These are no good for tanning and making clothes.

Elders also say in May and June, bulls develop another pouch the size of a small orange in the base of their throat. These bugs live there until they get big and then the caribou coughs them out. Elders say these bugs don't hurt the caribou. In fact, the caribou can't live without them. That's something interesting to know about male caribou. Someone who has caribou medicine could talk a long time about why the caribou and bugs need each other.

In the summer there are some fish in Barren Lands lakes, but come winter the shallow water freezes so people depend on caribou for food. Caribou are on the move all the time; sometimes people have a hard time to find them in that vast country. But they still go, and in the winter it is often very hard.

I remember a couple of times we met Inuit from the coast and we were afraid of each other, but after meeting each other awhile we got along very well. Our languages were completely different so we had to make a lot of signs to each other. In those days, we didn't kiss to show we liked someone, we just rubbed noses. To the Inuit, rubbing noses was the same as a kiss.

There were so many tough times. Sometimes we women and children would have to stay on the tree line all summer. We made as much drymeat as we could and saved the caribou tongues for the trader to buy. In those days, traders were dealing not only in furs, but also caribou hide strip string or babiche, drymeat, fat, and tongues.

So we would often stay home on the treeline while our husbands and older sons made the one hundred-mile trip to Behcho Ko in the fall. It would take them a month or so to get there and back; they had to travel from lake to lake and on so many small rivers. All this while they were packing heavy meat on their backs. The many portages were very hard work.

Some of us women learned how to shoot those early guns we had—muzzle loaders—so if a grizzly bear bothered us we could shoot it. Sometimes we shot caribou also. We were on our own a great deal, but we managed to survive. We kept busy getting food and making caribou hide winter clothes for our families.

When I was a young woman, before you could buy canvas up here, I made two caribou hide tipis. Four of my daughters helped me make the first one, out of twenty good hides we had tanned with no maggot holes in them. We lived for many years in that tipi in the Barren Lands. Caribou hide tipis are very warm because the hide is so strong and thick.

No one had invented mosquito repellent at that time, but we found ways to sleep comfortably in the spring when mosquitoes were very bad. We would put heavy moss all around the bottom of the tent until there was no way a mosquito could get in. We closed the door tightly and put rotten wood on the fire inside to smoke all night. The smoke drifts up out of the opening in the top—mosquitoes won't come in through that.

When the men finally returned from the trading post they would bring us a few special things like sugar, oats, and maybe some cloth. We all worked so hard back then.

A TRAPPER'S MEMORIES

Joe Wedzin of Behcho Ko (Fort Rae) is eighty years old as he tells this story of his travels and life in the bush.

I remember, as a teenager, living on a fish lake between Behcho Ko and Liidli Koe (Fort Simpson). There were about twenty families living there together and we didn't know much about the outside world. We went a few times to Behcho Ko, about 150 miles away, to trade our furs. I saw two white traders there, and one priest. We got what we needed for our furs—matches, powder, and balls for our muzzle-loader guns, tea, and maybe a blanket. The stores didn't have much more than that in those days.

We didn't know what was happening in the outside world, so we didn't feel like we were missing anything. We didn't worry much, we tried to live our life and be as happy as possible.

My father and I trapped with dogs packing our supplies, along with another father and his son who was about my age. We were so poor, our dads owned only five bullets each. The traders gave us only five bullets to last all winter. They didn't have much in their trading posts either so they rationed bullets and powder so everyone could have some.

If you miss the caribou or moose you're aiming at, you have to look for that bullet in the snow until you find it, that's how it was.

Our dads made us good bows and arrows for killing ducks, spruce chicken, and rabbits. We hunted as we travelled. It was a lot of fun for us teenagers.

We owned only five steel leg-hold traps; we used them for catching mink. Our fathers taught us how to make deadfall traps for fox and marten. This is a structure with a small, one-way door with a stick sticking out holding bait. When the animal pulls at the bait it triggers a load of wood and this drops on the animal and kills it.

Sometimes we would be out trapping for a week or so, hunting along the way. We did not even have a small tent, we just slept under a tree with a caribou hide for a blanket.

The elders are good hunters because they have been doing it for so long. They are good at tracking moose and woodland caribou. I remember when someone got one we would build a good hut out of spruce logs and smoke some of the meat to take home in the dog packs. The rest of the meat we would cache in a small house made of timber so the wolverine would not steal it from us.

We usually carried a fish net and we always worked our way towards an inland fish lake. We put the net under the ice and caught fish. So, our culture worked very well. You never had to starve if you worked right and lived off the land.

We had time to make two trips in the fall to visit our traps before Christmas. Christmas was a big thing in our culture. People from all directions would go to Behcho Ko at Christmas to see each other. We would go to church together and have a couple of tea dances and feast together and play handgames.

No one had any cash in those days. No one had very much, not the Dene, the traders, or the church. We lived so far away from the south where all these trade goods came from; everything had to be rationed. The traders were really careful about giving out hardware and food, like flour. You gave them your fur and you got a few things for it. The traders squeezed a profit from these poor people by buying fur cheap and selling items at three times more than they paid for them. That's how the Hudson's Bay Company made its money in the North country.

In the early 1900s the Dene were losing their medicine power. They started to depend on others to give them what they needed, like the traders, and on people who made a lot of promises to them, like the missionaries. Our whole lifestyle changed and we stopped depending on medicine power. Later, we depended on the government.

The early missionaries started to teach the Dene about their ways and tried to convert them. The Dene reacted quickly because they already had knowledge of a Creator who made the Mother Earth for them. Some priests were very hard on the Dene, saying their beliefs came from the devil and "if you don't convert, when you die you will go to a scary place." So, we believed them.

Soon the priests said "you have to give something to God" and since there was no cash, the people gave fish, dried fish, drymeat, caribou tongue, moccasins, caribou hides, and they gave fur to pay for a mass sometimes. The early priests became like traders. The Dene didn't know they were being cheated because they didn't know about business. They always shared whatever they had with other people, so they thought they were just sharing with the church.

People became very religious. They would travel hundreds of miles to go to church at Christmas and Easter. After Christmas, trappers would go back onto the land from February to March to get enough fur to go to Behcho Ko again for Easter, to celebrate and get the things they need again.

On the spring hunt, people killed beaver and muskrat. They really loved this time of the year. They moved their families to a good spot and enjoyed the noise of the wild ducks returning from the south. They ate well and, after all the cold weather, they were really happy because it was warm again. After the hunt, they would move back to their fish lake and the men would go to Behcho Ko to trade their furs again.

All summer, we would make a lot of dried fish and sometimes, if we were lucky, we would kill a moose or woodland caribou on the lakeshore.

Before the traders and the government came to Denendeh, people were poor and worked hard, but there was no disease and no violence; that was after great medicine people like Yamoria had cleaned things up. We governed ourselves with Dene laws and we kept our children in line by the elders teaching them each day. People lived a long time and they were happy. Problems started when outside people started to bother the Dene. Then their lives started to change and they started to worry more.

THE FLU EPIDEMIC

(Reprinted with permission from Nahecho Keh, Our Elders, *published in 1987 by the Slavey Research Project, Fort Providence, Northwest Territories)*

Jimmy Sabourin, of Zhati Koe (Fort Providence), was five years old when the 1928 flu epidemic killed one sixth of the Dene population. The loss of most of his family greatly saddened him, yet his spiritual beliefs helped him to accept the devastation.

My father said to me, "Once the snow melts we will break camp and go to town on the scow." As the weather grew warmer I used to climb aboard and I was amazed. I just couldn't imagine travelling on it at all! My father's mother, my granny, made me a little paddle and said it was for me so I could help my father.

When it was time to go, we loaded all our pelts and possessions onto the boat and set off. We drifted downstream and didn't even have to paddle. My father spotted a bear on the shore and he shot it. He and his older brother, Charles, took the canoe and paddled off to get it. When they returned granny noticed the bear had no ears. They looked as though they had been cut off with a knife. Everyone was very shocked and granny said it was a bad omen. We wanted to throw the carcass away but granny said we must wait and throw it away on dry land. When we came to shore for the night, the men cut the bear's stomach open and threw the carcass away into the bush.

It was spring time then so the days were long. My father had seen a moose and went off to hunt it. I went along to carry the knife. When we tracked the moose down, I went to look at its ear first. One of them was ripped down the middle. Again we thought it was a bad omen. It took all night to cut up the moose and haul the meat to camp. I helped too.

When we got to town, we opened up our house. We even had a stove in it. My family were great trappers and had good luck. The men went to the trading post in town that had just opened up. When they came back they had bought a gramophone. We were astounded and stood around the table listening to it all day.

Now the treaty payments were about to begin and the fields were covered with tipis. There were so many people! The sickness came so suddenly. What could we do? We couldn't even run away. Gabriel Denetre's father was drumming to ask the sickness to go back to where it came from. By the next morning hardly anyone could stand.

I saw the brothers driving a cart pulled by two cows. There were boxes on it, but I didn't know why. When Jean Marie Sabourin came in, I asked him and he said they were for the dead. I was really scared then.

My parents were too sick to even move. They couldn't even sip water and, of course, there was no medicine. Granny asked me to get her some manure to boil. She said it was powerful medicine.

I looked where my father had tied the dogs the previous year and found some.

I was trying to light the fire for her when the trader's children Maurice, Louie, Alphonse, and their sister Margaret came to help me. Granny tried to crawl out but she was too weak. We helped her put the manure in a lard pail, pour in water and set it on the fire. The children went back to their father and returned with some dried milk. They had things like that because their father was a white man. They mixed it with water and gave it to granny. She also drank the manure broth.

The priest, the grey nuns, and the brothers brought around watery oats and dried bread. They said it was for whoever was hungry.

I started to get sick that night. My ears began to buzz and my head hurt. The next morning I was hungry but I didn't know where any food was. Jean Marie found something for me: drymeat, fish, and a trout. He spoke to my parents. My father said he couldn't eat as he had a pain in his side. Jean Marie said he wanted to go back downriver but he couldn't. He was needed to dig graves. There was no one to help him. He was covered with mud.

My father said, "What is happening?" Then Jean Marie said, "Your brother died yesterday." When my father heard that, he started screaming and crying. He and his brother had been the only two sons in that family.

"How is my sister Liza?" he asked. Jean Marie answered, "She is sick."

I noticed granny was not moving. I told my father and he took off her blanket. She was no longer breathing. Even though he was so sick, my father laid her out himself.

When the priest came by, my father told him what had happened. The priest said, "There have been so many people dying. The brothers will make a coffin for her and come and get her." Then he prayed over granny with his rosary and blessed her with water. He said, "When you die, your body returns to dust, but your breath and soul belong to Jesus."

I was so sad and there were tears in my eyes. Who could I call granny now?

My father said that we would not burn her blankets, but leave them the way they were. I wasn't scared, not after what the priest said. That night I went and laid my head on her blankets and fell asleep. The next morning I was better. I believed that my granny had helped me get well and that made me happy.

Maurice and the other boys came by then and told me they had found something in the bushes and that I should go with them to see. It was a tent that had belonged to an old man who had died. Inside was a piece of white cloth on a pole with caribou antlers and a drum. There were also birchbark baskets and pans that you use for washing your face. The boys took the drum but I thought it might be dangerous. Maurice said he had heard the old man play his drum and he knew how to do it.

We went down to the river bank and Maurice drummed for us and we danced. I asked him if he drummed medicine songs but he didn't know. They were just songs that he could remember.

When we went to the fields, there was not one tipi left. The police had advised people to leave because of the epidemic. Many things had been abandoned in the rush to get away; knives and beautifully made baskets.

I sometimes think how I may well have been one of those put into a box and yet I survived . . . and here I am still walking around today.

LIVING THE DENE LAWS

This is a story about Suzie Bruno, eighty-five, of Behcho Ko, who tells about eight months in his life when he worked tirelessly to take care of a group of elders in the Barren Lands. He is a good example of someone who lived according to the Dene law that says, "Young people should always look after their elders."

At the present time I am very old, can't even cook for myself. The things I have done to help my elders are just a memory. Some people say work and be happy when you are young. They are right. I am glad I did this. I will tell you a story of how I worked in one year of tough living in the Barren Lands.

We used August 15 as a mark when we had to be deep in the Barren Land country hunting caribou. If we found caribou, we feasted on August 15—it was our culture to do this.

That fall, when it began to get cold, we were out of supplies so people prepared to make the three hundred-mile round trip to trade meat and hide at Behcho Ko (Fort Rae) to get tea, shells, and matches. It took them three weeks to get back, over long portages and many lakes, and by that time there was snow all over the land. Then, almost half of our group went back into the bush to trap marten and mink. So, there were not many of us still out in the Barren Lands. The caribou kept moving and we had to travel one or two nights at a time to hunt them. They were skinny that year and we had a hard time to feed ourselves and our dogs.

It got so bad, more people left for the bush land to find fish lakes, and soon there were only about five families still left in the tundra. There was my wife and I and four elders who couldn't work hard. We were in a place far from the main tree line. There was a patch of big willows and a few trees, not much for good firewood. To get firewood, we had to travel about five miles, and it was getting colder everyday.

We had a lot of drymeat but no fish. I was a young man, I slept very little: I had to hunt all the time. My wife was young too, and she worked hard with me. We had four elders—they were poor and their dogs were weak so they couldn't hunt far or work every day.

One of the things that got us through that winter was my good dogs. I had seven young dogs and I would use four at a time and leave three behind. My wife used those three to pack wood for her, and she fed them well. When I got back from a trip, I would exchange my tired dogs for her fresh ones.

The old people helped us too. They talked to us and encouraged us every day, reminding us to be good people and we said the rosary together every morning and evening, even though we were so busy.

With only me hunting, it took three or four nights to get back from the tundra with fresh meat. We almost starved once when I came back empty-handed, but then I went in a different direction the next time and got six caribou. That meat didn't go far between six people and by this time the dogs were getting no meat, only broth.

We lost track of time and we passed the Christmas season there in the Barren Lands. By March we were still just getting by; then the caribou moved north so we decided to follow them. Just the two old men went with me because the dogs were too weak to pull toboggans. We left a lot of meat with the two elderly women and my wife because we knew we might be away for as long as three weeks.

The men stayed in my main camp to fatten up the dogs while I hunted. We made better time getting back to the women with the dogs fattened up a bit better now. When we got back, the elders said it was time to move back to a fish lake in the bush country to join the rest of our people.

The days were getting longer and the sun was warm by the middle of the day. The elders joked and laughed, some of them sang their songs. We had made it through the winter eating only meat and drinking broth. Our clothes were in poor condition and we had no soap to wash with. The March weather made us snow blind and our skin was dark from windburn and the sun. We were in rough shape but we were happy to be back with our people.

Now, I sit alone with no wife, surrounded by my grandchildren of modern time. Their attitude toward each other is terrible, no manners or love at all. No sharing, everyone talks English, they watch TV, no one listens to parents or elders—they gave up teaching children so they have no direction; they are free to do whatever they want.

There's a court in place every week here in Behcho Ko. Young people go to jail regularly—mostly alcohol-related crimes like impaired driving. A lot of fines are set, but no one has money to pay so they go to jail.

These attitudes of our young people really affect me. When I was younger I worked hard and steady, and no one gave me twenty five cents. Yet I was happy. I didn't feel the work because I was young. I'm glad I did this for my elders; it's something to feel good about right now. But now I sit in a house alone, and it's not a good life.

Chapter Twelve

INTO THE

FUTURE

THE EARLY 1900S

Even though medicine powers were complex and could make life unpredictable for my ancestors, compared to today, daily affairs then were pretty uncomplicated. People spent their time hunting, fishing, gathering wood, building canoes and sleds, tanning hides, cooking and looking after children. Knowledge of the land, animal migratory patterns, and weather trends had to be extensive for survival, but in today's "information age" you have to know 100 times as much.

Elders, including myself, find the present fast-paced and out of control. We come from a time when our culture was healthy and we knew our place in the universe. We respected the land and animals and lived in balance on our Mother Earth. Our lives were hard but we were satisfied with small victories and minimal comforts. We didn't know any other way.

Our families and friends gave us joy and our connection to the Creator gave us a great sense of well-being. When my parents walked up a hill and broke into song to thank the Creator for their lives, it was a special thing. All life was sacred.

It's hard for us older Dene to change even though everything around us has changed. We know how to live life well in a certain way and we do not see our children living that way. If I were to walk up to a group of teenagers hanging around a pizza joint in Yellowknife and say, "Why don't you go out on the land and kill a moose? The experience of killing it, and eating the fresh meat, will be much better for you than this pizza," I imagine they would just look at me as if I were a crazy old man.

Outsiders might wonder why we elders still laugh and joke a lot, even though things are so bad. It's because we remember one of the most important Dene laws: As long as you see the land, it will always feed you and take care of you. Life is short, so make the most of it and don't worry. Be as happy as you can!

For a lot of elders and middle-aged Dene, this law is part of our mind, body, and spirit. That is why we are the way we are. We were educated within the extended family, and our elders taught us how to make a good life and to be good leaders for our people. We were taught to listen to each other, love each other, respect each other, and always help others to lead a good life. We came together every summer for a feast and tea dance, and we told stories about what we had done that winter.

Yellowknife Indians scraping moose hide, Stoney Lake 1955.

Modern life is not all bad. Babies have a better chance of surviving, medicine helps us live longer, and education and job salaries allow my children to live a much more comfortable life than I did at their age. But the balance is gone. The sacredness is gone.

Our sons, daughters, and grandchildren eat food from a package or can; they don't get strong from eating good, lean wild meat and nutritious broth. They have different attitudes toward sex and relationships. Many speak only English and they place more importance on the white culture they see on television than on Dene culture. Young people are spoiled by the conveniences of modern life. They want to have all the luxuries, but they have no way to earn the money to pay for them.

No one makes a living off the land anymore. There aren't many jobs in our small communities, so many still depend on government welfare. It's not good for a man or woman to sit idle every day. Their self-esteem suffers and when boredom sets in they often turn to alcohol or gambling. They shift their focus from raising their children well to self-destruction and trying to numb the pain of their disconnectedness. Young people drink, do drugs, and get in trouble with the law when they have nothing to do.

This splitting off from our identity as Dene began in the late 1800s and early 1900s. The fur trade and European settlement of the North changed us, but it was the mission schools that really upset our way of life. Since before history, the family was the heart of Dene culture. In the family we learned about life. Everything went in a circle—the older ones taught the younger ones, and then the younger ones eventually replaced the elders.

In 1920, the government passed a law that all children between the ages of seven and fifteen had to attend school. After that many were sent away from their families to attend boarding schools run by the churches. The government wanted our children to become civilized in a white way and to fit into its idea of how society should be.

Girls from mission school dressed for pageant as angels.

Students were taught academic subjects and the Christian religion, but they weren't allowed to speak their languages and they didn't receive enough love growing up. Everyone needs love and to feel they are worth something to someone. I don't think our children got this in the mission schools. You can't look after so many children all together and make each one feel special. Our young ones were raised by priests and nuns who had never had any children themselves and didn't understand our way of life. For a few people, the schools did them good, but for most others it shattered their spirit. The family circle was broken and our spirituality devalued by the dominant society.

SIGNING OF TREATY 11

After oil was discovered near Tulit'a (Fort Norman) around 1914, everyone began to notice the North. As people moved in to stake their claims, the federal government in Ottawa knew it had better do something to make sure it had title to the land that was being developed.

Until then, no one really bothered about who owned what and we Dene were free to travel and hunt wherever we wanted. So now government officials were sent to have our chiefs sign Treaty 11, but then a big misunderstanding occurred. We wanted to have the right to hunt and fish on our land forever, for our children to learn to read and write, and to have medical services.

Our chiefs couldn't read the agreements they were asked to sign. They understood that the treaty was like a goodwill agreement that these rights would be protected from the outsiders and the industry that was moving in. We didn't realize that, for five dollar annual treaty payments, a few schools, and some medical care, we would be permitted to hunt only where the government said we could. In signing Treaty 11, we didn't realize we were giving up our traditional rights.

After we signed, big changes came. Our Dene customs and traditions were gradually taken over by government law, enforced by police. People found themselves in courts for things they didn't know were wrong. Outsiders came North to make quick money trapping, threatening to destroy our way of life. They had no respect for the land and the ongoing life of animals. Our elders had told us to kill only what we need so the animals could repopulate and there would always be enough, but these people didn't care about that.

As competition between fur companies increased, we asked the government to stop newcomers from taking over our lands and trapping and hunting too much. Meanwhile, the government responded to official reports that the wildlife population was decreasing in the north by restricting where and how much we could hunt.

Dene who had always followed the caribou into the Yukon were told they now needed a "nonresident hunting license" to do so. Even though most didn't follow these regulations, the government was starting to control our way of life more and more and these laws had an increasing impact on us as the years went by. For

(Photo: ComPics International Inc.)

A peaceful evening at Bathurst Inlet.

the first time in our lives, we had competition and restrictions on the way we had always made a living.

The great flu epidemics of the 1920s helped weaken the ties we had to our spiritual ways. Many of our elders died and we lost great teachers who reminded us of our Dene way of life. Medicine power was snuffed out and it looked as though the white way was the only way.

Ottawa was introducing more and more laws—even though the politicians who made them lived in eastern cities and had no idea of what life was like in Denendeh. The RCMP enforced these laws and this took away even more of our identity and independent spirit.

Schools were built in our communities and we were told our children had to attend. The health department wanted our children to be educated so they could understand how to take care of themselves and stop the white diseases that had killed so many of us. All of a sudden we couldn't go out into the bush to hunt anymore because we had to stay in town while our kids went to school.

LOSING CONTROL

W e realized we needed some kind of help so we started to orga-
nize ourselves and initiate meetings with government agencies. The
officials' answer was to give us social assistance, money to help us
buy good food for our children and to pay our rent. Welfare helped
us in the short term, but it eventually left my people feeling even
more dependent, bored, and worthless.

No longer were the Dene strong and self-reliant as their ancestors had been, instead they counted on a monthly cheque from
social services. Jobs were scarce because companies didn't want to
hire native people, and the price of fur was low. Our self-esteem was
gone and we lived in despair.

When the government decided to legalize alcohol for native
people in 1958, we started on thirty years of heartbreak and pain.
Many Dene couldn't cope with all of the changes and were stripped
of their dignity, so they turned to the bottle to numb the pain.
Things were so bad we could only endure and wait for them to get
better. And slowly, they did.

By 1970 our children had been attending school for thirty
years. We elders watched them become educated so they could
play the complicated games of negotiating and claiming what was
theirs from the government. At the time when the treaties were
signed, many chiefs did not speak English and their attitude and
thinking concentrated on their traditional way of living according
to Dene law and culture.

When the young people told us they wanted to confront the federal government regarding the Dene view of Treaty 11, many elders were troubled. They believe no one owns the land, but that the Dene were put here to take care of it and have certain rights to it. The Creator made the land for everyone to share.

In the oral version of the treaty we understood that we never gave up any of the rights we had. After the written version was translated, the elders said it was untrue. Land was never discussed. Land tenure in Denendeh was never fully defined, yet the government has gained millions of dollars in revenues of which the Dene have seen no benefits.

CLAIMING OUR LAND

In the late 1960s, James Wah-Shee, president of the Indian Brotherhood, began to talk to chiefs who were present at the treaty signing of 1926. He hired lawyer Gerald Sutton to begin gathering the elders' testimony and presented it to the Territorial Supreme Court, along with a 720,000 square kilometres land claim to the western portion of the Northwest Territories.

Slave River rapids.

Though the case was lost on a technicality, we decided to press on. In 1978, the federal government's land claims proposal was rejected by both the Dene and Metis and stalled. In 1980, the newly-named Dene Nation (formerly the Indian Brotherhood) again began researching their position on the Dene/Metis claims and devised an in-depth aboriginal rights negotiations position.

In 1991, a few of the regions decided to go their separate ways and take up individual land claims. The Gwich'in in the far North have settled their claim, as have the Sahtu Dene. We Dogrib are still negotiating because we have so many issues in our region—mining, building dams, and setting boundaries—to consider.

The Treaty 8 Group, which includes communities south of Tucho (Great Slave Lake) and the Yellowknives of Dettah and Ndilo, are still negotiating and the Deh Cho region is also pursuing its own separate territory.

Farther North, the Inuvialuits and the Tungavik Federation of Nunavut have both settled their claims and have received land and cash compensation.

The total land involved in these negotiations covers half of the land mass of the whole of Canada. More importantly, these agreements move us toward implementing our inherent right of self-government and into a partnership with the government that will give us more control over our destiny than we've had for decades. As each claim is settled, we acquire the tools to become self-sufficient and self-sustaining. We are at last becoming major players in activities happening in our region.

MAKING THE BEST OF LAND
AND MONEY

haven't been sitting at the negotiation table, but I am encouraged by what I hear from those who have settled. For many reasons, we Dene haven't been managers of our lands or had any input in programs established for us. People who really knew nothing about us were making our decisions for us.

Some people have become quite content with letting the government look after them—receiving free housing, welfare, and other services. Now that they are owners of vast amounts of land and must deal with large amounts of cash, though, more and more they are taking responsibility for their lives. People who used to drink heavily have quit and now work for their people.

Some or all of the regions plan to come together on a major joint venture project in Denendeh to boost our economy. This land is rich and diverse, and holds much opportunity. I hope to see aboriginal people, who know Denendeh and its secrets so well, controlling many enterprising ventures in ways that comply with the Dene law of respect for people and land and animals.

Political and financial power gained from land claims settlement are positive steps toward a better life, but grassroots values of caring, sharing, respect, and love for each other also have to be part of the mix. And these virtues easily get lost when money and power are involved. Dene control of social, environmental, cultural, political, and economic affairs must be centred in the heart.

To make the best of the future, we have to work together to settle land claims and balance living in the modern world and returning to our culture. We have to revisit the treaty process and be compensated for the use of our land by the big oil and mining companies. At least thirty per cent of all jobs should be made available to the Dene.

Even with some good things happening for us, I still worry about how my people will cope with the future. We have so many challenges. The cost of living is high in the North and jobs are scarce, with up to eighty per cent unemployment amongst Dene. Our young people still aren't being hired by the large companies extracting resources from our land. Maybe the education they receive isn't good enough, or perhaps they are discriminated against.

The dependent relationship we have with the government of Canada is not good. It's been fifty years since government, education, and health services were established in Denendeh, but we seem to have more problems than ever.

We haven't responded to government help because we are still Dene. Despite attempts to assimilate us, we still have ancestral values. For example, to get jobs we often have to move to large centres like Yellowknife and Inuvik, but some families are reluctant to move there to work because they want to stay in their small communities near relatives.

Our country is huge and the climate is cold. We can't grow or hunt our own food anymore so we rely on a government that is deeply in debt and can't take care of us now. As our population increases, where will the services, housing, and money we will need come from?

Sometimes I think my people will have to change completely to the white way of doing things. Maybe when the present elders die the younger people will take over and live other kinds of lives. The old people don't want to change and they enourage young people to live the old way, so many young Dene are mixed up.

View of the dance, Fort Rae, NWT 1937.

I think we will need spiritual help to make it into the future. Today I hear some young people are receiving songs in their dreams. In ceremonies people sometimes "talk" to relatives in the spirit world who are communicating from the other side. I believe nothing is ever completely lost, it is just forgotten.

Because the earth has changed, and because we Dene do not live in the same way as our ancestors—eating only wild meat and living outdoors in the clean air—medicine is not the same as it was before. But we still have power. We have our imagination, our dreams, our virtues, and our faith in the Creator, and those are a medicine person's most important tools. May this book remind us of the strength of our ancestors, of our Dene laws, and to live the best way we know how.

BIOGRAPHIES

•••'·•••·••••••••••••••••'·•••

Behcho Ko (Fort Rae)

Suzie Bruno was born in 1907 in Rae-Edzo and was Grand Chief of the Dogrib people from 1969-1971. He is a storyteller who tells of the tough times trapping on the Barren Land area where there are no trees or wood to make fires. Suzie is the son of the longtime Grand Chief of the Dogrib people, Jimmy Bruno.

Jonas Lafferty was born in 1954 in Rae-Edzo. He is one of the official translators for the Rae Band and Treaty 11. His job takes him to many meetings, large and small, where he meets many people and picks up many good stories. Jonas is the son of Edward and Melanine Lafferty,

Alphonse Lemoule was born in 1914 in the Fort Rae region. He has lived a traditional life and has good knowledge of the land, medicine power and oral history. Alphonse is the son of powerful medicine people, Suzie and Julie Lemoule. He is a descendent in direct line from the 19th century Dogrib leader Edzo.

Joseph MacKenzie is a great storyteller and has been harvesting the land since childhood. He lived through a period when the Dene were very poor, often having to use animal skins for clothes for the winter. He has many stories about the start of the 19th century and when the world was new.

Joe Wedzin was born in 1942 and has lived most of his life in the town of Rae-Edzo. Joe is the son of Pierre and Elise Wedzin.

Pierre Wedzin was born in 1904 in Fort Rae. He lived most of his life in the bush and has accomplished much in his lifetime. He is a good story-teller, has seen a lot of traditional action and was once a chief of the Dogrib people. He is a co-founder of the Snare Lake village. Pierre is the son of Wedzin and Tawa.

Deline (Fort Franklin)

Edward Blondin was born in Fort Norman but travelled a lot. He was the grandson of Edwa Blondin, a very strong medicine power person, who adopted the name Blondin from a French trapper in 1870. The name Edwa is taken from a Dene tribe from Luxrux in the Delta. As a baby, Edward slept with his grandfather for three years and inherited his great medicine powers from him. A trapper and hunter all his life, Edward harvested the land from the Mackenzie Mountains to the Mackenzie River Delta and in the Great Bear Lake area. He married a girl from Great Bear Lake and was the father of George Blondin.

Julia Blondin was from Fort Franklin. She was the wife of George Blondin. George and Julia moved to Yellowknife in 1949, where Julia died in 1975. Julia was the daughter of Francis Ayha who was the son of the great Prophet Ayha of Deline.

Joe Nadzo spent all his life as a trapper around the Great Bear Lake. He spent a lot of time around Indian gathering places for he told many stories. He was a good person and was well respected by many people. Joe was the son of the prophet named Nadzo.

Deninu (Fort Resolution)

Edward Lafferty, a Metis, is a good trapper and has trapped most of his life. He also has worked for the white people of Deninu. He knows all the elders in that area and has many stories. Edward is the father of Jonas Lafferty.

Gene Norn is a good trapper who travelled a lot around the Deninu area and knows a lot of people and saw a lot of traditional action and picked up many stories. Elder Norn has also worked for many white people that came into that country.

Radeli Ko (Fort Good Hope)

Ka Na Een was from Fort Good Hope originally but he travelled a lot in his lifetime and was at Collville Lake, Fort Norman, Fort Wrigley, Fort Franklin, and Fort Rae. He was a great man and a strong medicine power person who had the respect of all the people. He was a very good story teller and also talked about medicine power.

Tsoti (Lac La Martre)

Helen Rebesca was born in 1897 in Fort Rae and died in 1996, two weeks before her ninety-ninth birthday. She was a well-known Elder and storyteller who knew traditional medicine. She was married to Bruno Rebesca. Helen was the daughter of Yambi and Kowe'a.

Tulit'a (Fort Norman)

Fred Andrew is from Fort Norman, the son of a long time chief. He spent his teenage years around the Whitehorse area and much of his life in the mountain range between Mackenzie River and Yukon Terrritory where he harvested the mountain country for a living. He later ended up on Fort Norman. He is a great storyteller.

Zhati Zop (Fort Providence)

Jimmy Sabourin was born in 1923 at Red Knife. As a five year old he remembered the flu epidemic of 1928. For many summers he worked on the Hudson's Bay Company boats from Fort Smith to Aklavik, and the rest of the year he would trap.

PHOTO CREDITS

NeWest Press gratefully acknowledges the following for permission to use the photographs in this book—

Reverend Bernard W. Brown: Pages 27, 65, and 221

Aaron Herter: Page vii

Alberta Environmental Protection:
Recreation and Protected Areas Division:
Pages 55, 67, and 229

ComPics International Inc.: Ph: (403) 434-4075 Fax (403) 436-0494
E-mail: compics@compics.com Web Site: www.compics.com
Cover (Bathurst Inlet and Bear Rock), chapter title pages (Bathurst Inlet and caribou), pages 21, 49, 53, and 225

Edmonton Space and Science Centre:
Cover (northern lights) and page 45—Frank Florian photographer

Hudson's Bay Company Archives, Provincial Archives of Manitoba:
Cover and chapter title pages (lodges) (HBCA 1987/363-I-46/8 [N11689])
—Louis Roy photographer

National Archives of Canada:
Department of the Interior photographic collection:
Page 23 (PA.42048)
Charles A. Keefer:
Page 61 (PA.73748)—detail, 233 (PA.073759)—detail

NWT Archives:
R.S. Finnie:
Pages 25 (N1979-0063:0051) and 41 (N1979-063:0189)

The Provincial Archives of Alberta:
Ernest Brown photographic collection:
Pages 19 (B.779), 31 (B.2935), and 33 (B.2917)
O.M.I. photographic collection:
Cover and title page (children) (Ob.933) and page 37 (Ob.10762)

University of Alberta Archives:
Louis Romanet fonds:
Page 223 (Accession 72-81, Item 692)

Photo research: thanks to Debra Moore (Hudson's Bay Company Archives, Provincial Archives of Manitoba), Tina Sangris (N.W.T. Archives), and Carole Séguin (National Archives of Canada)